Piazza-style eating and shopping in Nelson Mandela Square

Johannesburg

the Bradt City Guide

Lizzie Williams

edition

I

www.bradtguides.com

Bradt Travel Guides Ltd, UK
The Globe Pequot Press Inc, USA

Johnnesburg city centre at dusk

(WK/IOA) page 142

Mural, Newtown (SA/IOA) page 144

Robert Broom holding skull of Mrs Ples, *Plesianthropus africanus*, Sterkfontein Cave (AZ) page 215

SA National Railway and Steam Museum (AZ)

Randburg waterfront

(AZ) page 129

Lion, *Panthera leo*,
Lion Park

(AZ) page 211

Blesbok, *Damasiscus dorcas*,
Krugersdorp Game Reserve

(AZ) page 209

Author

Lizzie Williams (*www.writeafrica.co.za*). Originally from London, Lizzie has worked and lived in Africa for 12 years, starting as an expedition leader on trips across the continent on overland trucks. She has travelled to over 20 African countries and is now something of an expert on border crossings and African beer. She is author of several guidebooks including the first country-specific guidebook to Nigeria, the *Bradt Guide to Nigeria*. Amongst other websites, she has written www.overlandafrica.com, a leading website on the overland industry in Africa, and has contributed Africa destination guides to US websites including *tripz* and *yahoo*. Lizzie writes full time and when not on the road lives in sleepy (according to Jo'burgers) Cape Town.

First published January 2007

Bradt Travel Guides Ltd
23 High Street, Chalfont St Peter, Bucks SL9 9QE, England; www.bradtguides.com
Published in the US by The Globe Pequot Press Inc, 246 Goose Lane, PO Box 480,
Guilford, Connecticut 06437-0480

A catalogue record for this book is available from the British Library

ISBN-10: 1 84162 176 5   ISBN-13: 978 1 84162 176 0

Photographs Text Ariadne Van Zandbergen (AZ), Lizzie Williams (LW), Shaen Adey/Images of Africa
(SA/IOA), Walter Knirr/Images of Africa (WK/IOA)
Front cover Gold Reef City casino (WK/IOA)
Title page Newtown moral (SA/IOA), Nelson Mandela statue (LW)
Maps Steve Munns   **Illustrations** Carole Vincer

Typeset from the author's disk by Wakewing   Printed and bound in Spain by Grafo SA, Bilbao

Contents

Acknowledgements

Many thanks to all my friends in South Africa involved in the tourism industry, especially my 'family' in Jo'burg at the Backpackers Ritz; Steve, Mignon, Peter, Mark, Astrid and the whole tribe of little Baines's – it was great to spend time with you once again. Thanks also to Neo, for being a great guide in Soweto, all the helpful staff at the various tourist offices, and to the wonderful scribblers on www.joburg.org.za who pointed me in the right directions.

FEEDBACK REQUEST

In a modern, vibrant city such as Johannesburg, things change rapidly. Restaurants and hotels reinvent themselves, new establishments open their doors, and there is an ever increasing agenda of things to do and see. I would love to hear your recommendations and experiences. Write to Bradt Travel Guides, 23 High St, Chalfont St Peter, Bucks SL9 9QE or email info@bradtguides.com.

Introduction

Johannesburg, also known affectionately as Jo'burg or Jozi, is the bright star of southern Africa. Just look at a map and it seems all roads in sub-Saharan Africa lead to Johannesburg. It is the most densely populated and urbanised area in South Africa, with a population of just over three million. Estimates reckon that by 2015 Johannesburg, Pretoria and their satellite towns will have all joined up to make the resulting urban space the 12th largest city in the world. Jo'burg is also the economic powerhouse of Africa, built on one of the richest gold reefs in the world, which has attracted fortune seekers for the last hundred years. Today it's a pulsating, busy, working city which draws people from all over the continent still looking for fortune, hope and opportunity. The city is made up of sleek modern architecture, a tangle of highways, billboards, skyscrapers, townships, and 600 suburbs representing every socio-economic level. It is not too dissimilar to a large American city, and much like its recently declared sister city, New York, Johannesburg has always attracted diverse people and been a place of extremes; it's been everything from the best to the worst of cities since 1886.

Johannesburg is the cultural capital of South Africa and has a showcase of theatre, dance, township jazz, rock and pop, and some of the best restaurants and shopping opportunities on the African continent. It's an African city with plenty of action, where everything works smoothly, and where the city council is passionate and generous about the well-being of its residents. And these residents have a myriad of personalities, from the privileged *dolls* and *okes* with mobile phones permanently attached to their ears in the northern suburbs, to the upbeat informal traders on the vibrant streets of Soweto. A visit to an upmarket shopping mall and a tour of the townships contribute equally to understanding what modern South Africa is all about.

Yet Johannesburg has had a turbulent history. It was only in the 1980—90s that it emerged battered and bruised from the dark years of apartheid, and it has only recently come to terms with the effects of becoming a truly African city again.

During apartheid its neighbouring city Soweto didn't even feature on maps, despite being home to millions of people. The township represents the living, structural statement of South Africa's former political mind, where some of the most important, tragic and jubilant events occurred during the struggle against apartheid. It was once home to some of the country's favourite grandfathers, such as Nelson Mandela and Desmond Tutu; people that cared deeply about South Africa and have gone on to become some of the greatest statesmen in the world. Today Soweto is a living, breathing neighbourhood, and whilst poverty is still raw in the squatter camps on its periphery, there are large areas of Soweto with decent housing where residents can aspire to good healthcare, education and a hopeful future for their children.

Since the demise of apartheid, Johannesburg has had to deal with a tarnished reputation for high crime levels. Like elsewhere in the world, crime rears its ugly head when there are so many people in poverty trying to eke out a living. Johannesburg's crime problems are a result of the breakdown of apartheid in a period when the city was trying to heal and mend itself. Over a decade later, Johannesburg has become stronger, and has formulated forward-thinking policies to govern itself. Today it is addressing crime, health, education, welfare, and housing productively and successfully. Nothing happens overnight, but the vision and ambition of a city that wants to move away from the politically ravaged and dangerous place it once was, to a bright, modern, confident and intelligent world-class city that it has become, are more than evident.

The changes today are remarkable, and the efforts by the government, the Johannesburg municipality, the tourism authorities and private industry are laudable. Visit www.joburg.org.za, the city's website, to read about the very many various projects, plans, and absolute enthusiasm there is out there that is making Johannesburg a wonderful place to live in and visit again. In just over 100 years Johannesburg has grown from a mining camp, to an apartheid planner's utopia, to a menacing ghetto, and now it's ripening into Africa's Big Apple. Jozi rocks – enjoy.

How to Use this Book

PRICES in this guide were correct at the time of writing. Rates at hotels in Johannesburg are generally the same all year round, without seasonal hikes as in the rest of South Africa. Most have single and double rates. Restaurant prices include taxes but not tips – 10% for good service is about the going rate. On average in Johannesburg, a starter costs in the region of R35 and a main course R70, rising considerably in the more upmarket restaurants.

CREDIT CARDS Most establishments accept the full range of credit cards, though smaller museums or cafés may not. Note that the chip-and-pin system is gradually being introduced in South Africa.

OPENING HOURS Most restaurants open daily from 10.00 or 11.00 until late. They tend to double up as cafés and bars for snacks and drinks with more extensive menus for lunch and dinner. For the more popular ones, it is advisable to make a reservation. Museum opening hours are listed in the text, but check carefully as some close one day a week.

MAP REFERENCES (eg: [2 G1]) These relate to the colour map section at the end of the guide.

WEBSITES These are listed wherever possible so that readers can look at photographs and check current price. Many offer reliable booking online which often attracts a discount.

JOHANNESBURG AT A GLANCE

Location Lying on a high-altitude inland plateau at 1,753m above sea level in the northeast of South Africa (it takes a minute longer than at sea level to boil an egg here); 10½ hrs flying time from London, 14 from North America

Size 1,644km² with approximately 600 suburbs

Population 3,225,800

Language Eleven official languages, but English is spoken by nearly everyone

Religion Predominantly Christian, though just about every faith is represented

Time GMT + 2

International telephone code 027

Currency Rand (R) £1 = R13.99; US$1 = R7.33; €1 = R9.37 (November 2006)

Electricity 220v; 3 round pin plugs

Public holidays 1 January, New Year's Day; 21 March, Human Rights Day; Good Friday; Monday after Easter Sunday, Family Day; 27 April, Freedom Day; 1 May, Workers' Day; 16 June, Youth Day; 9 August, Women's Day; 24 September, Heritage Day; 16 December, Day of Reconciliation; 25 December, Christmas Day; 26 December, Day of Goodwill

Climate Summers are hot and wet with frequent electrical storms; winters are cool and dry with occasional frosts. If it is exceptionally windy, dust is blown off the mine dumps and creates a slight haze.

I Contexts

INTRODUCTION

Whilst not being the capital of South Africa (nearby Pretoria, 50km to the north and linked by a ribbon of development, holds that title) Johannesburg is the biggest city in the country and the largest city south of Cairo. It is also regarded as the financial capital of South Africa thanks to it being the largest producer of gold on earth (it has produced 40% of all the world's gold) and it's home to the biggest stock exchange on the continent. It's also the location of banking and financial institutions, pharmaceutical and electronic companies, and international importers and exporters that play a major role in trade all over Africa. For most South Africans this is the city where things happen – deals are done and careers are forged, and for many Africans from all over the continent, it's a destination where there is the possibility of employment and a better lifestyle for their families than what they would expect from their home countries. Indeed Jo'burgers, with their fast cars, sharp suits, and frenetic pace of life, couldn't be more different from their cousins in South Africa's other major city, Cape Town. There is much humour bantered around amongst South Africans on the differences between Jo'burgers and Capetonians. People living in Cape Town are supposedly terrible drivers, very sleepy, unambitious and spend too much time frolicking in their waves or walking up their mountain. Jo'burgers, on the other hand, drive too fast, are super ambitious and successful, but don't know how to relax, and live in a hard-hearted concrete jungle.

It is true that Johannesburg is predominantly a business city, and a very successful one at that. It hasn't been built next to a river or an impressive mountain, it's six hours' drive to the sea, and it may not have the scenic majesty of some of the other attractions in southern Africa. But it is a major gateway to Africa, and most travellers, whether they're here on business or pleasure, are likely to pass through; there are plenty of things to see and do, and it's rich in culture and modern African history. It also has some of the best infrastructure in Africa, with modern amenities, good telecommunications, a well-organised tourism industry and world-class service. Its varied attractions include an excellent line of museums, lots of green spaces, wildlife projects, cultural villages, theme parks and lively townships, not to mention mega shopping malls, a vibrant nightlife and award-winning restaurants. At least a few days of exploration is warranted to experience the Jozi vibe, and although weakened, the value of the rand against the £, €, and US$ still represents excellent value in South Africa for the visitor.

HISTORY

EARLY DAYS As the largest city in sub-Saharan Africa, Johannesburg – or *Egoli*, meaning 'place of gold' in Sesotho – is a surprisingly young city. In 1836, following a ban on the recruitment of slaves by the British administration, the Dutch-speaking farmers of the Cape, known as the Boers, were faced with almost inevitable financial ruin. In desperation, they packed up their wagons and headed north on what history has dubbed the Great Trek. Many of these people, known as the Voortrekers, settled in the Rand region of South Africa, later to become the Transvaal, intending to return to their traditional way of life founded on the family and the Bible. But this Old Testament kind of existence was transformed almost overnight by the discovery of gold in the Rand in 1885. Thousands of immigrants, or Uitlanders ('foreigners') as the Boers called them, swarmed into the Rand – miners, engineers, businessmen, prospectors and adventurers – all lured by the prospect of becoming rich from gold.

The Pretoria government laid out a plan for the town and Johannesburg rapidly grew into a city. It was named after two men, Johannes Meyer and Johannes Rissik, who both worked for the government in land surveying and mapping. As capital poured into Johannesburg, this proved to be the beginning of an industrial revolution, drawing Africans away from rural land and into new cities and towns. By 1895 almost 100,000 people lived in Johannesburg and the mines employed more than 75,000 workers. Confidence in the city was so great that traders from other regions of the country dismantled their buildings and moved lock, stock and barrel to the new city to set up shop. The Star newspaper relocated from Grahamstown and transported its printing press across the veld by ox-wagon. Riotous *shebeens* (pubs), gambling dens and brothels sprung up, and because of the inevitable brawls that occurred between men in pubs in the pioneering days, the first jail was built on

Johannesburg's first barmaid was Amanda Aquenza, employed by Mr Chas Brown in a bar in Ferreira's Camp. Here is an account of her eagerly awaited arrival in the town by E C Trelawney Ansell in his 1939 book *I Followed Gold*:

> I do not think that I shall ever forget the arrival of the first barmaid in Jo'burg. Word of her coming had got ahead of her. Tales were being spread of her wonderful beauty, the glorious clothes she wore, the very low cut of her bodices, etc. Special emphasis was also laid on how easily she bestowed her nightly favours – at a price. The day came when the coach was to arrive with this beauty of the bar. Crowds of the Jo'burg 'boys' were there to meet her. Cheer after cheer went up as she was carried shoulder high from the coach to the billiard room of the Central Hotel, there to be regaled with iced champagne.

Commissioner Street. Building went on all over the city and by the end of the 19th century railways, electricity and telephones had all arrived. The first gold share transaction to be registered on the Stock Exchange happened in a miner's tent in Ferreira's Camp in 1887. From the tent, business moved to Johannesburg's first stock exchange, Donovans' livery stables on the corner of Sauer and Commissioner streets, and then on to a brick building on Commissioner Street.

Less than ten years after the discovery of gold, the newcomers outnumbered the Boers in the Transvaal, controlling most of the wealth in the region. Despite this, neither the Boers nor the then Transvaal Prime Minister Paul Kruger wanted them to gain political control. A conference between Kruger and the British High Commissioner, Alfred Milner, achieved nothing, and in 1899 the Boer War began, affecting the whole country. The Boers were defeated by the British and fighting stopped in 1902. A peace deal was struck whereby the Boers were to surrender their independence, but the English and Dutch languages were to have equal status, and the Boers were granted a responsible government by 1907 in both the Transvaal and the Orange Free State. A year later the Constitution for South Africa was drafted, uniting the Boer and British colonies.

GROWTH OF A CITY The pace of change in Johannesburg from 1900 to the outbreak of World War II was faster and on a larger scale than anywhere else on the African continent. By 1939 the concentration of mines and factories was comparable to the industrial regions of Europe and North America. Gold flowed to the world's banking houses, binding South Africa into the international web of finance and commerce. Yet the fruits of this prosperity were unevenly distributed, especially amongst the Africans. The country's economy depended on the gold mines and the gold mines depended on African labour – yet by 1939, African miners and others in industrial jobs were earning only about an eighth of the wages paid to whites. Racial tensions became sharper as more and more Africans were integrated into the expanding economy.

After 1909 the mines began to obtain the bulk of their labour through the enrolment of migrant workers who came to Johannesburg from other parts of South Africa, Lesotho, Zimbabwe and Mozambique. Their families would stay at home whilst these men lived in hostel accommodation for eleven months of the year near the growing crop of gold mines. Compounds consisted of single-sex hostels housing between eight and sixteen men per room. Later complexes could house up to 5,000 workers each. Almost from the beginning, these living arrangements gave rise to a number of social problems. Alcohol abuse, venereal disease and prostitution were common amongst miners, and the general male–female ratio, which remained high right up to the late 1930s, didn't help matters. In 1902, for example, the total black population in Johannesburg was estimated at 64,700, of which only 7,600 were women.

As well as the hostels, black mine workers also lived in 'locations' or townships which first started to appear in the 1920s in such places as Newclare, Sophiatown, Prospect and the Malay Location. Johannesburg set up a Committee of Native Affairs in 1928. Before then the affairs of 'native administration' had been rather inexplicably handled by the Department of Parks and Recreation. Between 1936 and 1946 Johannesburg's black population grew by 59% to a total of nearly 400,000. During the same period the comparative growth of the white sector was 29%. A lack of housing meant that the majority of blacks were forced to move illegally into vacant tracts of land in such areas as Orlando, Pimville, Dube, Newclare and Alexandra, where squatter suburbs sprang up virtually overnight. Once in the townships many miners began to bring their families to the city, and the women and children increased the pressure upon an already overloaded informal infrastructure.

APARTHEID In 1948 the Herstigte (meaning 'reformed' or 'pure' in Afrikaans) National Party (HNP) came into power. Within a year the Mixed Marriages Act was instituted – the first of many segregationist laws devised to separate privileged white South Africans from the black African masses, and, by 1958, South Africa was completely entrenched in the philosophy of apartheid ('being apart'). There was opposition to the government's policies. The African National Congress (ANC) was working within the law against all forms of racial discrimination in South Africa. In 1956 it had committed itself to a South Africa which 'belongs to all.' A peaceful demonstration in June 1955, at which the ANC (and other anti-apartheid groups) approved the Freedom Charter, led to the arrest of 156 anti-apartheid leaders, and the subsequent Treason Trials lasted until 1961 and led to a number of imprisonments or exiles.

Pass laws were introduced, and blacks, Indians and coloureds were forcibly removed from Johannesburg's city centre to new and existing townships. It is this system that created sprawling Soweto, short for South West Township; the township for the blacks. Although building started here in 1904, it increased in size dramatically during the 1950s and 1960s, when, with a series of loans raised from Johannesburg's mining companies (most specifically Sir Ernest Oppenheimer of Anglo-American), the city council was able to fund the construction of houses. By

1958, 40 houses per day were being handed over, and by 1969 a total of 65,564 houses had been built in Soweto alone. In 1970 it was home to an estimated 1.2 million people (today its population is thought to be about 900,000).

Soweto was the brainchild of racist and segregationist thinking. When the residents of squatter camps were forcibly resettled in Soweto, there was no attempt to respect existing social structures and neighbourhood units. Instead these were wilfully split up, breaking the spirit of the community. Road access to Soweto was limited to three major routes to restrict movement in and out of the area in the event of civil insurgency. Street grids were designed in such a way to locate police stations and nests of machine-guns at the hubs in order to control any potential unrest. No provisions were made for the creation of business districts, or for industrial and manufacturing areas, and it wasn't until the 1980s that the township got electricity and running water. Soweto was the spawn of apartheid, and its location, planning and architecture served as a constant reminder of this fact to its residents.

Soweto played an important part in the fight against apartheid and was home to many of the leading activists, including Nelson Mandela and Archbishop Desmond Tutu, who once lived in the same street in Orlando West – the only street in the world that was home to two Nobel Peace Prize winners. In 1976 Soweto experienced serious student riots, now known as the Soweto Uprising, sparked by a ruling that Afrikaans was to be the primary language used in African schools. The riots were violently suppressed, with 176 people killed and more than 1,000 injured.

TRIUMPH

One of the more infamous forced removals during the early years of apartheid was that from a suburb called Sophiatown, which had originally been a vibrant centre in which many races lived alongside each other in relative calm. In the 1940s there was a huge cultural explosion of jazz music and art in Sophiatown, which attracted African writers and artists and a number of Bohemian whites. The government bulldozed it and forced out the residents in much the same manner as they razed District Six to the ground in Cape Town in 1966. They had to destroy it; it simply proved that residents of different races could live together. A new white suburb was built in its place, rather crudely called Triomf, Afrikaans for Triumph. In 2006, the name of the suburb was changed back to Sophiatown.

The police openly fired on defenceless schoolchildren, a story that made headlines and raised awareness of what was going on in South Africa around the world and changed the course of South African history. The famous photograph of the lifeless body of the 13-year-old Hector Pieterson being carried by mourning youths (see page 179), symbolises the 1976 uprisings and the earnest step-up of the struggle against apartheid. In Soweto the anger of the youth grew tremendously; there were further protests well into the 1980s, and the amount of violence, vandalism and gang-related crimes increased dramatically. These gangs were regularly attacked by

NELSON MANDELA

1963 Leader of the African National Congress (ANC), Mandela is arrested at Lilieslief Farm in Rivonia, for sabotage, and sentenced to life in prison on Robben Island.

1976 Mandela is approached by Jimmy Kruger, the Minister for Police serving under President B J Vorster, to renounce the struggle and settle in the Transkei. Mandela refuses.

1982 With growing international pressure against the South African government to release Mandela and his compatriots, P W Botha, arranges for Mandela and Walter Sisulu to be transferred back to the mainland to Pollsmoor Prison, near Cape Town.

1986 Mandela is taken to see the Minister of Justice, Kobie Coetzee, who requests once again that he renounce violence in order to win his freedom. Despite Mandela's refusal, restrictions on his liberty are somewhat lifted: he is allowed visits from his family, and is even driven around Cape Town by the prison warder.

1988 Mandela is diagnosed with tuberculosis. On release from hospital he is moved to 'secure quarters' at Victor Verster Prison near Paarl.

1989 Things are looking bleak for the apartheid regime; P W Botha has a stroke, and shortly after meeting Mandela at the Tuynhuys, the presidential residence in Cape Town, he resigns. F W de Klerk is appointed as his successor and meets with Mandela.

1990 At the opening of parliament (2 February) De Klerk announces the un-banning of all political parties and the release of political prisoners (except those guilty of violent crimes). On 11 February 1990 Nelson Mandela is finally released.

1991 The Convention for a Democratic South Africa, CODESA, is set up to negotiate constitutional change. Both Mandela and De Klerk are key figures in the negotiations.

1993 Mandela and De Klerk jointly win the Nobel Peace Prize.

1994 The first multi-party, multi-racial elections in South Africa are won by the ANC with a 62% majority. Mandela makes his inaugural presidential speech from the Union Building, Pretoria. Shortly after, he publishes his autobiography, *Long Walk to Freedom*.

1996 Mandela and his estranged wife, Winnie Madikizela-Mandela, divorce.

1997 Mandela steps down as leader of the ANC in favour of Thabo Mbeki.

1998 Prompted by Archbishop Desmond Tutu, Nelson Mandela and Graça Machel, the widow of Mozambique's former president, marry on Mandela's 80th birthday.

1999 Mandela retires as president and is replaced by Mbeki. After his retirement he becomes an advocate for a variety of social and human rights organisations.

2003 Mandela supports the 46664 AIDS fundraising campaign.

2004 In the year that marks ten years of democracy, Mandela is awarded Freedom of the City of Johannesburg. At the age of 85, he retires from public life except for his commitment to the fight against AIDS; his son died of AIDS in 2005.

2005 *Time* magazine lists Nelson Mandela as one of the top four people in history to have shaped the 20th century.

the police and Soweto became a bi-word for terror, poverty, and injustice. This reputation in a way helped South Africa in the long run and heightened the world's awareness of the horrors of apartheid.

Between 1950 and 1970 there were further incidents that fuelled the struggle in other areas of Johannesburg. In 1963, on Lilieslief Farm in Rivonia, Walter Sisulu and others from the ANC were arrested. Nelson Mandela (already arrested the year before in Natal) was brought to Pretoria to join them and they were charged with 200 counts of 'sabotage, preparing for guerrilla warfare, and preparing an armed invasion of South Africa'. The trial later became known as the Rivonia Trials. Mandela was one of five out of ten of the activists to be given a life sentence, and that year he began his 27-year incarceration on Robben Island in Cape Town.

On 21 March 1960, 69 blacks were killed and at least 180 were injured when South African police opened fire on approximately 300 demonstrators who were protesting against the pass laws at the township of Sharpeville, near Vereeniging to the south of Johannesburg. In similar demonstrations at the police station in Vanderbijlpark, another person was shot. Later that day at Langa, a township outside Cape Town, police baton charged and fired tear gas at gathered protesters, shooting three dead and injuring several others. The Sharpeville Massacre, as the event became known, signalled the start of armed resistance in South Africa and the ANC adopted terrorist strategies. Within 18 months of the Sharpeville Massacre the ANC's armed wing had sabotaged over 200 government installations.

In the 1980s, people took the liberation struggle to new heights, and all areas of life became areas of political struggle. There were frequent protests, both violent and peaceful, and community organisations such as women's groups and student and youth organisations began to spring up all over South Africa. International pressure was strong in the way of sanctions, demonstrations against apartheid outside South African embassies abroad, and even rock stars using their voices to speak out about South African injustice (perhaps most famously the rock band U2). 1989 was the year in which the logjam started to break up. Negotiations had been entered into between Mandela and P W Botha (although in secret at first). Dissension within the Nationalist Party, in combination with Botha's ill health, led to his resignation and he was replaced by F W de Klerk. After an election in September, De Klerk released Walter Sisulu and seven other political prisoners. Then, at the opening of parliament in February 1990, De Klerk un-banned all political parties and released all non-violent political prisoners. Nelson Mandela became a free man on 11 February 1990, and went on to become the first black president of South Africa (see box on page 10).

URBAN DECAY For Johannesburg the end of apartheid had a very unusual and dramatic effect on the city. Pass laws had already been banished since 1986 and since then black South Africans had been able to choose where they lived and were no longer restricted to the townships. Black people moved back into the city centre and to the suburbs that were once whites-only enclaves such as Yeoville, Hillbrow and Berea. The 1990s also saw a huge, largely unchecked immigration surge of Africans from other countries north of South Africa all the way up to Morocco. As the blacks moved in, the whites moved out and retreated to the affluent northern suburbs of Sandton, Rosebank, Randberg, Rivonia, Parkhurst and Melville, where they still today lead increasingly paranoid lives in houses with alarms and high walls protected by razor wire. There was also a 'white flight' from the country after the 1994 elections as the more conservative whites, unsure where the new black government would steer the country, literally took flight to Canada, the UK, Australia and New Zealand. The city centre was transformed from a sleek, modern grid of office blocks, to a vibrant, lively authentic African city with a clamouring street life, not dissimilar to Nairobi or Dar es Salaam, though sadly not without a new set of problems.

The crime rate in the city centre soared. This was due mainly to illegal immigrants without legal status to work in the country, and the unemployed turning to crime to make a living. It was also the inevitable consequence of the widespread changes in South Africa during a time which necessitated a complete overhaul of the country's laws and institutions (so that they would be aligned to the new constitution), and a restructuring of the police service from eleven separate agencies into one unified body, with responsibility to the whole nation.

In Johannesburg centre, Rocky Street in Yeoville became a war zone with drive-by shootings and car jackings; the high-rise apartment blocks in Hillbrow became a hangout for drug lords and prostitutes; and there were frequent muggings and mobile phone snatchings downtown and in the Newtown precinct. Hillbrow is still bad: an inner city slum that has one of the highest population densities in the whole of Africa. Many of the buildings, owned by absentee landlords, teeter on the edge of collapse and serve as crack cocaine dens or brothels. It is probably the most feared neighbourhood in the country.

The result of all this was that businesses packed up shop, moved out of the city centre and relocated to new business parks and shopping malls in the northern suburbs. The Holiday Inn, the Stock Exchange, the Carlton Hotel, even the post office, all closed or moved out. Most of the skyscrapers were left standing empty with evidence of broken windows, vandalism and squatting. Completely derelict former office blocks were converted into illegal housing, with no central management and more often than not no water, electricity, waste disposal or other basic amenities. The original owners abandoned their properties and failed to pay local rates, and the new illegal tenants lived in abject poverty in buildings that had been hijacked by slum landlords. The city had its guts ripped out, and by the mid 1990s was an abandoned and lawless place that had been dubbed one of the world's most dangerous cities and the murder capital of the world.

URBAN RENEWAL In recent years things have improved greatly. The Central Johannesburg Partnership (CJP) (*www.cjp.co.za*) was created in 1998 as a private, non-profit company focusing on the revitalisation of the city. It has set up numerous City Improvement Districts where the property owners agree to pay for certain services to enhance the physical and social environment of the area. These include extra policing, security patrol officers, CCTV cameras, pavement cleaning, litter control, and maintenance of public spaces. The CJP has also been instrumental in clearing up 12 inner city parks and finding accommodation for the homeless that used to use them. Irrigation and fountains have been fixed, fences mended and children's playgrounds built. It has also been revitalising squares and pedestrianising certain streets to form attractive precincts, and has completely revamped the Newtown precinct, which is again alive with restaurants, museums, art galleries and theatres. Private industry too started to realise that it was also responsible for Jo'burg's revival and ABSA bank made the ground-breaking move of building their new, R400 million headquarters in the city centre.

The police, too, are cracking down on drugs and firearms, and have ousted whole apartment blocks of illegal immigrants. A new police force, known as the Metro Police, was created in 2001 specifically for the city centre. This is a force of 4,000, which also monitors over 350 CCTV cameras throughout the city. Other significant improvements include the national amnesty of guns in June 2005, which saw 80,000 firearms handed in to the police countrywide. The murder rate decreased by 37% between 1994 and 2004, and Johannesburg is certainly not the murder capital of the world any more. Vehicle theft, including car jacking, is down by 30% during the same period and the number of robberies and robberies with aggravating circumstances also showed significant declines. The CCTV cameras have been exceptionally successful in reducing street crime.

The city council has identified 94 'bad buildings' in the centre of Johannesburg. Bad buildings are buildings that have been invaded by slum landlords and tenants, and whose amenities have rapidly deteriorated to the point where they cannot cope with the demands placed on them. The owner often absconds when these conditions become overwhelming, leaving huge amounts of unpaid rates owed to the city council. In 2005 the inner city revival further gathered pace when the National Treasury declared much of Jo'burg's inner city as the country's largest Urban Development Zone. This project entitles building owners who refurbish their properties to a tax incentive and a write-off of unpaid rates, or alternatively buildings are expropriated and offered to new investors. By August 2005, the city council had received applications from property owners and investors for more than R1 billion worth of improvements. Since then, and at the time of writing, 19 buildings have been refurbished and another 48 expropriated and acquired by new investors. This has caused a ripple effect, and there are now another 100 or so buildings being refurbished by private owners that are not on the 'bad buildings' list. Slum landlords who are operating overcrowded and rundown buildings, even where the rates and service payments are being paid, are being identified and urged to rehabilitate their buildings and bring them under proper management. If they prove to be obstinate, a 'naming and shaming' strategy is being considered.

In 2003 Johannesburg was 'twinned' with New York City in the US. Recent rejuvenation of this city too has been tremendous: violent crimes in New York have dropped by over two thirds in the last decade and the FBI reports that murder rates are now at their lowest since 1967. The comparison between the two sister cities is poignant. Both had terrible reputations in the 1970–90s but now, with governments and councils that are enthusiastic about healing the problems of inner city strife, they are becoming-world class cities again. The policies of the various authorities are clear – to lower the crime rate and to make New York and Johannesburg's inner city a safe and attractive place where people can live, work and play.

THE FUTURE Johannesburg is big and bold, and the time for investment is ripe. The city centre should soon become be a safe, clean and pleasant place to visit again and vast improvements are underway. In 2006 some R178 million was allocated to community health services to boost the city's HIV/AIDS programme, and the city aims to build 200,000 houses for the poor over the next ten years. The new R7 billion Gautrain Rapid Rail Link currently under construction will link Johannesburg with Pretoria, 50km to the north, via the airport, and will create almost 100,000 jobs. Experts predict that by 2015, Johannesburg, Pretoria and their satellite towns will have become a single mega-city, the 12th largest in the world. The FIFA 2010 World Cup, which has been awarded to South Africa, will also enhance the city, and the opening match, one of the semi-finals and the final will be held in Johannesburg, spawning huge investment in tourism development. Currently 52% of tourists to South Africa spend some time in Johannesburg, and, by 2010, it is estimated that visitors to South Africa will exceed 10 million annually.

POLITICS

In April 1994, South Africa got its first democratically elected leader, President Nelson Mandela, and the ANC won its first non-racial elections. Mandela formed a

Government of National Unity, that he ran for five years whilst a new constitution was drawn up, which was adopted in 1996. South Africa was accepted back into the Commonwealth, all remaining sanctions against the country were lifted, and it took a seat in the UN General Assembly after a 20-year absence. In 1996 the Truth and Reconciliation Commission, chaired by Archbishop Desmond Tutu, began hearings on human rights crimes committed by the former government and liberation movements during the apartheid era. The report that was published in 1998 branded apartheid as a crime against humanity, but also found the ANC accountable for human rights abuses during their period of armed struggle. The ANC again won the 1999 elections and Thabo Mbeki took over as president. He again won the 2004 elections but had to sack his deputy, Jacob Zuma, in the aftermath of a corruption case. South Africans are due to go to the polls for the next general election in April 2009, but under the constitution Mbeki is not permitted to stand for a third time.

ECONOMY

Although Johannesburg built its wealth on gold, the last active gold mine shut down in 1979, which is today Gold Reef City (see page 196). The city's infamous gold dumps are today being slowly cleared to make way for new development, though it's believed a couple will remain as reminders of the city's history. However, the legacy of gold has worked like a Midas touch, and today Johannesburg is easily the most economically powerful city in Africa. It generates 16% of South Africa's wealth

JOHANNESBURG'S FAMOUS GRANDPARENTS

ARCHBISHOP DESMOND TUTU Born in 1913, Tutu is an Anglican cleric who over the years has consistently been one of the most outspoken critics of apartheid. In 1978 he became the first black general secretary of the South African Council of Churches, and in 1984 was awarded the Nobel Peace Prize for his role as a unifying leader in the campaign against apartheid. He headed up the Truth and Reconciliation Commission in the late 1990s, which played an important role in healing the wounds inflicted by the former regime.

JOE SLOVO Born in 1926 in Lithuania, the white activist moved to Johannesburg as a child, went on to become a member of the South African Communist Party, and was involved in drafting the Freedom Charter in 1955, and the establishment of the ANC's armed wing, *Umkhonto we Sizwe* (MK). He lived in exile from 1963 to 1990, but continued to fight for liberation from overseas. He died in 1995.

WALTER AND ALBERTINA SISULU Walter, born in 1912, and Albertina, born in 1918, were leading activists for the ANC. Walter was the founding member of the ANC Youth League in 1944, and along with Mandela and many others was sentenced in the Treason

and employs 12% of the workforce, in industries from finance and insurance to heavy industry and mining. Johannesburg also has the most skilled workforce in the

Trials of 1963 and sent to Robben Island. He was released from prison in 1989 and went on to become deputy president of the ANC in 1991. Walter died in 2003. Throughout her husband's imprisonment, Albertina played a crucial role in the ANC.

F W DE KLERK Born in 1936, De Klerk entered politics in 1972 and became leader of the National Party, and later the last white president of South Africa (in 1989). He was one of the main architects of South Africa's constitutional democracy and promoted a negotiated end to apartheid, which jointly with Nelson Mandela earned him the 1993 Noble Peace Prize. He retired from politics in 1997.

OLIVER TAMBO Born in 1917 in the Eastern Cape, Tambo went to Johannesburg, where he became one of the founding members of the ANC Youth League in 1944. He went on to become deputy president of the ANC in 1958, and finally president in 1985. During this time he was exiled abroad and mobilised international opposition to the apartheid system, including targeting the United Nations, and by 1990 the ANC had acquired missions in 27 countries. He returned to South Africa in 1991 and died in 1993.

country, with a 20% advantage over the rest of the country in terms of literacy and numeracy skills. Johannesburg lies in South Africa's smallest and wealthiest province,

Gauteng, meaning 'place of gold' in Sotho, which generates 38% of the country's GDP, and 9% of the whole African continent's GDP. Johannesburg's freight terminal, linked to the sea at Durban harbour by rail, handles 30% of Africa's exports and is classed as the fifth-largest freight-handling depot in the world. The city is home to the Johannesburg Securities Exchange, the biggest stock exchange in Africa and the 16th biggest in the world. In the 2006 budget it was announced that South Africa's economy was developing by 5–6% annually which is by far the highest growth of any African country. Also, in 2006 foreign investment was up by 70% compared to what it was in 2003, and tourism was up by 10% compared to 2004. Tourism alone now attracts an income for South Africa of over R100 billion annually.

PEOPLE

Research results show Johannesburg as the most prosperous place to live in Africa, and the standard of living is higher here for both the black and white population than the rest of South Africa and sub-Saharan Africa. Of the 3.2 million population, black Africans comprise 73%, whites 16%, and the remaining 11% are Indian, coloured, and Asian. Johannesburg is home to 7% of South Africa's total population. According to the last census in 2001, Johannesburg has just over a million households with an average of 3.2 people per household, though 12% of households are home to six or more people. Jo'burgers are relatively young, and 50% of the population is under 35 years of age.

BUSINESS

Gauteng is South Africa's economic powerhouse, so it is no mystery that a large percentage of visitors to the province arrive to conduct some sort of business. Johannesburg is completely geared up for business and just about every international company operates there. There are state-of-the-art conference facilities, most hotels have business centres, and wireless internet has arrived. Mobile phones can be hired at the airport and SIM cards are available everywhere. Johannesburg business people tend to dress more formally than in the rest of the country; men and women wear suits or at least a smart shirt. There are plenty of spots for power breakfasts or lunches in the northern suburbs and meetings often take place over a meal.

RELIGION

Most religions are represented in South Africa and there are numerous mosques, synagogues and churches. Most church-going whites with an Afrikaner background attend the Dutch Reformed Church. At least 75% of Africans have been influenced by Christianity (mostly Protestant) though a few have been converted to Islam, and there is even a tiny minority of black Jews. Black church attendees belong to regular or Zionist churches. Soweto is also home to a large Catholic cathedral that played a pivotal role for the community in the struggle against apartheid, and was stormed by the police during the Soweto Uprising when children took refuge inside (see page 162).

2 Planning

THE CITY – A PRACTICAL OVERVIEW

The Greater Johannesburg Metropolitan Area is a sprawling city of around 600 suburbs covering about 1,300km². This makes it the largest city in Africa in size, though not in population. It's roughly 100km across from Randfontein in the east to Nigel in the west, and some 60km from Midrand in the north to Vosloorus in the south. The city is neatly bounded by a ring road of freeways, mostly made up of the N1 which goes to both Pretoria and Cape Town, the N12 that goes to both Nelspruit and Kimberley, and the N3 to Durban. Within this boundary the high-rise city centre lies to the south and the northern suburbs to the north, mostly clustered around Sandton, where many of the businesses, shops and offices relocated to when things turned sour in the old city centre. Whilst the northern suburbs contain houses, shopping malls, parks and leafy streets, Sandton itself is another clutch of albeit very smart skyscrapers, so effectively the skyline of Johannesburg is broken by two sets of high-rise buildings and has two city centres. OR Tambo International Airport is to the northeast, about midway to Pretoria and accessed off the R21. Over the years, the 50km stretch of the N1 highway between Johannesburg and Pretoria has seen much development and it won't be long before these two cities are completely joined up. To the southwest of the N1 and outside the ring road lies Soweto, from where a steady stream of minibus taxis bring workers into the city and home again each day. Through the centre of the circle made up by the N1, N12 and N3, the two major highways linking all regions of the city are the M1 that runs north to south (from the N1 north of Sandton to the N12 near Soweto), and the M2 (which runs along the south side of the city centre from the N12 to the N3).

There are no accommodation options left in the city centre so visitors will most likely find themselves around the airport or in the northern suburbs on arrival, as this is where all the hotels are located. Getting around Johannesburg isn't easy as there are large distances to cover and it really is a city designed for cars. The public transport system is inadequate and whilst there are thousands of minibus taxis and a network of metro trains serving commuters, these aren't generally recommended for visitors. If you don't want to drive yourself, there are plenty of half- and full-day tours on offer that will show you all the sights and will pick up and drop off at your hotel.

WHEN TO VISIT *Weather Bureau* ☎ 082 162

Johannesburg is located on a high plateau 1,753m above sea level and has a reasonably temperate climate. Summers from November to February are hot, with long sunny days, temperatures averaging 25°C and no humidity. This is also the

FNB DANCE UMBRELLA *Feb;* ☏ *011 482 4140; www.at.artslink.co.za*
A three-week festival of contemporary choreography and dance from community-based dance troupes to international companies, held at various venues around the city.

THE RAND SHOW *Apr;* ☏ *011 661 4000; www.randshow.co.za*
This attracts up to 500,000 people over two weeks on 51,000ha of space in and around the Expo Centre. There's everything from kids' events, musical concerts and dancing, to stunt shows, art and sport; something for everyone.

JOY OF JAZZ *Aug;* ☏ *011 636 1858; www.joyofjazz.co.za*
Annual jazz festival with over 200 local and international performers playing at different venues across the city, particularly in Newtown.

ARTS ALIVE *Sep;* ☏ *011 268 2577; www.artsalive.co.za*
A four-day festival with over 600 performers in dance, visual art, poetry and music at venues mainly focused in the inner city area and Newtown. This has previously hosted US rap stars.

WOODSTOCK *Sep;* ☏ *011 646 6467; www.woodstock.co.za*
Held at Hartbeespoort Dam, this is a four-day youth-orientated music and lifestyle festival, with lots of local bands and camping, similar to a weekend country rock festival in Europe.

wettest time of year, and there are some violent electrical storms and hail storms that can cause brief flooding on the roads, although these usually occur during the afternoon and clear up quickly when the sun comes out again. Spring and autumn are warm and clear and show the city's trees at their best: blooms in spring and warm golden hues in autumn. Winters are relatively short and dry with a cold snap of a few weeks over July and August when there are occasional frosts. During this time daytime temperatures rarely rise above 17°C and can be as low as 4°C at night, so this may not be the best time to visit. For some unfathomable reason, despite these temperatures South Africa has never really got to grips with the concept of central heating or double glazing. You may need to ask for an extra blanket on a cool night.

Most of Johannesburg's attractions can be visited whatever the weather, though obviously the parks or the zoo are far nicer on a sunny day, while the museums can be saved for a rainy day.

HIGHLIGHTS

ONE DAY

- Spend the morning on a thought-provoking tour of Soweto, singularly the most popular attraction in Johannesburg.
- Spend the afternoon soaking up the whole story in the superb Apartheid Museum.

- Sip a sundowner on the terrace of the Westcliffe Hotel and enjoy the great views.
- Treat yourself to a gourmet dinner and fine South African wines at an award-winning restaurant – *Yum* or *Moyo*.
- Late night party goers should head for the stylish bars in Melville, where there's something for everyone.

TWO DAYS *(in addition to the above)*

- Take a morning tour of downtown Jo'burg, which includes a visit to Museum Africa and the newly vamped Newtown precinct.
- Imagine what life was like for early miners at Gold Reef City and drop down a 220m shaft.
- Shop until you drop in one of the city's many malls. Glide with the super models and Sandton housewives in Sandton City.
- Try out the best South African melt-in-your-mouth steaks at the Butcher Shop & Grill.
- Sit with a nightcap and people-watch in Sandton's Nelson Mandela Square.

THREE DAYS *(in addition to the above)*

- Breakfast al fresco and browse the African curio market at Rosebank Mall.
- Take the lunchtime excursion to the all singing and dancing Lesedi Cultural Village.
- Have a close encounter with lions and cuddle a cub at the Lion Park.

- Head for the Newtown precinct to gawp at the new Nelson Mandela Bridge lit up at night, and for a traditional African meal at Gramadoelas.
- Check out live performances at the Market Theatre.

i TOURIST INFORMATION

The **South African Tourist Board** (℡ *011 895 3000; www.southafrica.net*) has to be one of the most efficient and organised tourist authorities in the world. It has an excellent website with information, maps and latest travel news, plus airline and accommodation options. It is published in 13 languages and covers how to get to South Africa from each highlighted destination. The tourist board also has representatives around the world:

Australia 117 York St, Sydney, NSW; ℡ +61 2 926 15000; e bangu@southafrica.net
France 61 Rue La Boetie, 75008 Paris; ℡ +33 1 456 10197; e info.fr@southafrica.net
Germany Friedensstr 6–10, Frankfurt 60311; ℡ +49 69 929 1250; e info.de@southafrica.net
India 44 Maker Chambers, Jamnalal Bajaj marg, Mumbai 400021; ℡ 0991 22 22850409;
e india@southafrica.net
Italy Via Mascheroni, 19, 5th Floor, 20145 Milano; ℡ +39 02 4391 1765; e info.it@southafrica.net
Japan Akasaka Lions Building, 1-1-2 Moto Akasaka, Minato-Ku, Tokyo; ℡ +81 3 347 87601;
e info@southafricantourism.or.jp
Netherlands Jozef Isralskade 48 A, 1027 SB Amsterdam; ℡ +31 20 4713181; e info.nl@southafrica.net

UK 6 Alt Gr, Wimbledon, London SW19 4DZ; ☏ 0870 155 0044; e info.uk@southafrica.net
USA 500 5th Av, 20th Floor, Suite 2040, New York; ☏ +1 212 7302929; e newyork@southafrica.net

Gauteng Tourism Authority (GTA) (*www.gauteng.net*) is the provincial tourism board covering Johannesburg and Pretoria and their satellite towns. Its HQ has recently moved into the Newtown precinct.

Newtown corner 1 Central Pl, Henry Nxumalo and Jeppe Sts, opposite Mary Fitzgerald Sq, Newtown; ☏ 011 832 2780; *open Mon–Fri 09.00–17.00*
International Airport ☏ 011 390 3602/14; *open daily 06.00–22.00*
Rosebank Craft Market ☏ 011 390 3614; *open daily 09.00–18.00*
Sandton City ☏ 011 784 9597; *open daily 09.00–18.00*

Johannesburg Tourism (*Ground Floor, Grosvenor Corner, 195 Jan Smuts Av, Parktown North;* ☏ *011 214 0700; www.joburgtourism.com; open Mon–Fri 08.00–17.00, Sat 09.00–13.00*) is doing a superb job at promoting the city and has a very comprehensive website. There are several other websites for information on the city; see page 227.

INTERNATIONAL TOUR OPERATORS

The South African Tourist Board lists all tour operators specialising in South Africa. Visit *www.southafrica.net* and click on your country of residence.

Recommended tour operators include:

UK AND IRELAND

Aardvark ✎ 01980 849160; www.aardvarksafaris.com
Abercrombie & Kent ✎ 01242 547700; www.abercrombiekent.co.uk
Acacia Adventure Holidays ✎ 020 7706 4700; www.acacia-africa.com
African Odyssey ✎ 01242 224482; www.africanodyssey.co.uk
Africa Travel Centre ✎ 0845 450 1541; www.africatravel.co.uk
Bailey Robinson ✎ 01488 689 2290; www.baileyrobinson.com
Baobab Travel ✎ 01902 558 316; www.baobabtravel.com
Cazenove & Loyd ✎ 020 7384 2332; www.cazloyd.com
Expert Africa ✎ 020 8232 9777; www.expertafrica.co.uk
Global Village ✎ 0870 999 484; www.globalvillage-travel.com
Imagine Africa ✎ 020 7228 5655; www.imagineafrica.co.uk
Okavango Tours & Safaris ✎ 020 8343 3283; www.okavango.com
Rainbow Tours ✎ 020 7226 1004; www.rainbowtours.co.uk
South African Affair ✎ 020 7381 5222; www.southafricanaffair.com
Steppes Africa ✎ 01285 650011; www.steppesafrica.co.uk

USA

Adventure Centre ✎ +1 800 228 8747; www.adventurecenter.com
Africa Adventure Company ✎ +1 800 882 9453, ✎ +1 954 491 8877; www.africa-adventure.com

AUSTRALIA AND NEW ZEALAND

Africa Exclusive ☎ +61 7 547 48160; www.africaexclusive.com
Classic Safari Company ☎ +61 300 130 218; www.classicsafaricompany.com.au
Peregrine Travel ☎ +613 8601 4444; www.peregrine.net.au

RED TAPE

Most nationalities do not need visas to travel to South Africa, including EU nationalities and travellers from the US, Australia and New Zealand. You must have a valid passport that is still valid for up to six months after your departure from South Africa. On arrival you will be given a 90-day visitor's permit. You can extend this at the Department of Home Affairs in Johannesburg (☎ *011 836 3228; www.home-affairs.gov.za* [5 E6]), and in the other offices around the country, but you will need proof of funds (such as a credit card) and an onward plane ticket from South Africa.

The official customs allowance for visitors over 18 years is 200 cigarettes, 50 cigars, 250g of tobacco, two litres of wine, one litre of spirits, 50ml of perfume and 250ml of toilet water. Tourists are restricted to bringing in R5,000 of South African rand from their home country. If you are coming from a yellow-fever infected country, you will be requested to show your yellow fever vaccination certificate on arrival. If you don't have one, you will have to have the vaccination in the airport's medical centre before being allowed to enter the country.

SOUTH AFRICAN EMBASSIES AND CONSULATES

Australia corner Rhodes Pl and State Circle, Canberra; ✎ 02 627 32424; www.sahc.org.au

Belgium Rue de la Loi 26, Wetstraat 26, Brussels; ✎ 02 285 4400; www.southafrica.be

Canada 15 Sussex Dr, Ottawa; ✎ 613 7440 330; www.southafrica-canada.ca

Denmark Gammel Vartov VEJ, No 8, 2900 Hellerup, Copenhagen; ✎ 039 180 155; www.southafrica.dk

France 59 Quai d'Orsay, Paris; ✎ 01 535 92323; www.afriquesud.net

Germany Tiergartenstr 18, Berlin; ✎ 030 220 730; www.suedafrika.org

Israel Yakhin House, Top Tower, 50 Dizengoff St, Tel Aviv; ✎ 03 525 2566; www.safis.co.il

Italy Via Tanaro 14, Rome; ✎ 06 852 54262; www.sudafrica.it

Japan 414 Zenkyoren Bld, Hirakawa-cho, Chiyoda-ku, Tokyo; ✎ 03 3265 3366; www.rsatk.com

Netherlands 40 Wassenaarseweg 2596 CJ, The Hague; ✎ 070 310 5920; www.zuidafrika.nl

Spain Edificio Lista, Calle de Claudio Coello 91, Madrid; ✎ 91 436 3780; www.sudafrica.com

Sweden Linngatan 78, 11523 Stockholm; ✎ 08 243 950; www.southafricanemb.se

Switzerland Rue du Rhone 65, Geneva; ✎ 022 849 5454; www.missions.itu.int

UK South Africa House, Trafalgar Square, London; ✎ 020 745 17299; www.southafricahouse.com

USA 3051 Massachusetts Av NW, Washington; ✎ 0202 2324 400; www.saembassy.org; there are also consulates in Los Angeles and New York

TRAVEL INSURANCE

Before departure, it is vital to take out fully comprehensive travel insurance. At the very least, the policy should cover medical expenses, including the possibility of medical evacuation by air ambulance to your own country, and personal effects. Johannesburg has excellent healthcare facilities but they are very expensive and in most cases you will have to pay up front or at least prove that you will be able to pay bills. In case of emergency, the Mediclinic (*www.mediclinic.co.za*) private hospitals in Johannesburg are recommended and there are many branches around the city.

GETTING THERE AND AWAY

✈ **BY AIR** Johannesburg is one of the most important hubs for air travel in the southern hemisphere and the airport is served by 45 airlines, with more than 11 million passengers passing through each year. There are numerous daily flights from Europe, North America, Asia and Australia, and there is a vast choice of routes and flights, but for the best fares you need to book three to four months in advance, especially over Christmas. Very usefully most flights to and from Europe go comfortably

NAME CHANGE

On October 27 2006, Johannesburg International Airport was renamed OR Tambo International Airport in honour of Oliver Reginald Tambo who spent most of his life serving in the struggle against apartheid and was among the founding members of the ANC Youth League.

overnight and the timings mean your days aren't eaten into by flights. Jetlag is also not an issue as there is a minimal time difference with Europe, so although the flights are fairly long (10½ hours) you are not going to be too frazzled at the other end. Johannesburg is served by all of the African airlines so regional air travel is easy to organise.

OR Tambo International Airport is modern and efficient with food courts, shops, banks, ATMs, post offices, car and mobile phone rental desks, and shuttle bus services into the city and to the hotels. You can also hire porters to help with your luggage, and if you are just passing through in transit and have a few hours to kill, there's a spa and gym across the road at the Intercontinental which can be used by non-guests of the hotel. There's also a hotel within the airport above the duty free shops for those in transit (see page 76).

Although there are some direct flights to Cape Town, the majority of international flights arrive in Johannesburg, before connecting to the other cities in South Africa. This means immigration is done at Johannesburg regardless of your final destination. Despite having loads of desks in the immigration hall there can be lengthy queues when a couple of 747s unload at the same time, though the airport has recently employed 40 extra immigration officials to ease the situation. For onward flights, you need to pick up your bags and then check in again at the domestic terminal. Remember to put locks on your luggage – there have been many incidents of wandering hands by baggage handlers at Johannesburg airport. Information on airport facilities and flight arrivals: ☏ 086 727 7888; www.airports.co.za.

From Europe British Airways (*www.britishairways.com*), Virgin (*www.virgin-atlantic.com*), and South African Airways (*www.flysaa.com*), are the main operators with daily flights between London Gatwick and Heathrow and Johannesburg. Nationwide (*www.flynationwide.co.za*) is a regional carrier in southern Africa but has one daily flight between Johannesburg and London Gatwick. Other European carriers include Air France, Air Portugal, Alitalia, Austrian Airlines, Iberia, Lufthansa, KLM, and Swiss International. Indirect flights from other airlines can also represent good value. Kenya Airways (*www.kenya-airways.com*) flies between London and Johannesburg, via Nairobi; Air Namibia (*www.airnamibia.com.na*) between Frankfurt and London to Johannesburg and Cape Town via Windhoek; and Emirates (*www.emirates.com*) daily to Johannesburg via Dubai from just about everywhere else in the world.

From North America South African Airways code shares with Delta and has daily direct flights between Johannesburg and Atlanta (about 17 hours) where you can connect to New York and other cities. American Airlines has a code share agreement with British Airways for flights to Johannesburg and Cape Town via London Heathrow.

From Australia, New Zealand and Asia South African Airways code shares with Qantas on flights between Johannesburg and Perth (10 hours), where you can connect on to the other Australian cities. Singapore Airlines (*www.singaporeair.com*) has flights between Sydney and Johannesburg via Singapore, and have a code sharing agreement with Air New Zealand, so those flying from Wellington to Johannesburg will have two changes *en route*. Malaysia Airlines (*www.malaysia-airlines.com*) flies from Perth, Melbourne, Sydney and Darwin in Australia, and Auckland in New Zealand, to Kuala Lumpur, to connect to the Johannesburg flights. Cathay Pacific (*www.cathaypacific.com*) flies to/from Johannesburg from Hong Kong.

 BY BUS There are three main coach companies and one backpackers' bus that cover South Africa and most services go via Johannesburg. Some have services that go over the borders between Johannesburg and Blantyre, Bulawayo, Harare, Lusaka, Gaborone, Maputo, Windhoek, and Livingstone in Zambia (via Namibia). All bus tickets can be booked online or through **Computicket** *(Rosebank mall, Sandton City, Montecasino mall, and Eastgate mall:* ✆ *083 909 0909; www.computicket.com)*. The long-distance bus station is in the city centre at the Park City Transit Centre on Rissik Street, which is also home to the railway station. This is a modern structure which gets very busy, so at all times keep hold of your luggage and don't go out of the complex and on to the street. You can pick up a taxi easily enough, and most of the hotels and backpackers can arrange transfers. All the bus companies have waiting lounges and there are a number of cafés and fast-food joints.

The Baz Bus is a hop-on, hop-off bus that offers a convenient and sociable alternative to the main bus companies. It is specifically designed for backpackers visiting South Africa and remains one of the most popular ways of seeing the country on a budget. The bus collects and drops off passengers at their chosen backpackers' hostel. Visit the website for the full timetable and fares.

Baz Bus ☏ 021 439 2323; www.bazbus.com
Greyhound ☏ 012 323 1154; www.greyhound.co.za
Intercape ☏ 012 380 4400; www.intercape.co.za
Translux ☏ 011 774 333; www.translux.co.za

🚗 **BY CAR** There are several border crossings from neighbouring countries within striking distance of Johannesburg and in total South Africa has 55 border crossings. The major ones are reasonably efficient with long opening hours, some 24 hours. In most cases you are able to take a hire car freely between South Africa, Botswana and Namibia as these countries are part of the Southern African Development Community (SADC) which shares the same customs union. You will need a letter of permission from the hire company to take a car across the border – simply fill in the details of the car registration in a book at the border post. These days most hire companies don't allow you to take a car into Zimbabwe, though some will permit you to go into Mozambique.

From Gaborone in **Botswana**, the main border crossings into South Africa are at Pioneer Gate, Ramatlabana and Tlokweng Gate. From all three you can follow the N4 to Pretoria and Johannesburg. The most direct route between Johannesburg and **Namibia** is via Botswana. The road between Johannesburg and Maputo in **Mozambique** has improved considerably due to the new toll road between Nelspruit and Maputo via the border at Komatipoort. Visas for Mozambique are available at the border and cost US$25. Border posts between South Africa and

Swaziland are at Ngwenya, Lavumisa and Mahamba. The N17 heads from Johannesburg to Ermelo, from where there is direct access to these three border crossings. The only border crossing between **Zimbabwe** and South Africa is at Beitbridge, just north of Musina at the end of the N1. The Department of Home Affairs in Pretoria can provide up-to-date details of the opening and closing times of border posts (☏ *012 810 8911; www.home-affairs.gov.za*).

🚂 **BY TRAIN** There are several passenger trains that criss-cross South Africa and almost all the services go through Johannesburg. The railway station is in the Park City Transit Centre in the city centre. There are daily services to and from East London, Musina, Komatipoort, Bloemfontein, Durban, Cape Town and Port Elizabeth. There used to be a train to Harare in Zimbabwe but this is no longer the case. Whilst the trains are both reasonably comfortable and affordable, with adequate sleeping compartments (though the food is rather bland in the dining cars), there are lots of stops and they are incredibly slow. Painstakingly so. The journey from Cape Town to Johannesburg takes about 27 hours, compared to $16^{1}/_{2}$ hours by bus, and around 14 hours by car. For information, timetables, fares and online bookings, contact Spoornet (☏ *0860 008 888; www.spoornet.co.za*).

BY LUXURY TRAIN South Africa's luxury trains operate much like five-star hotels on wheels and are a wonderful experience. Service is impeccable, the sleeping compartments are very comfortable, and the dining cars, bars and salons very atmospheric. All run regular scheduled services between Pretoria and Cape Town via Johannesburg and usually take one full day and night.

The Blue Train ☏ 021 334 8459; www.bluetrain.co.za
The Pride of Africa operated by Rovos Rail; ☏ 012 315 8242; www.rovos.co.za
Union Limited Steam Rail Tours ☏ 021 449 4391; www.transnetheritagefoundation.co.za

✚ HEALTH with Dr Felicity Nicholson

There are no serious or unusual health risks in Johannesburg. Although not mandatory, as for all travel it is a good idea to be up to date with basic vaccinations including tetanus, diphtheria and polio. Tap water is fine to drink and standards of hygiene are high. Be aware, though, that South Africa is top of the list in the world's HIV/AIDS rates so abstain or practise safe sex. Also be aware of the sun, which is more intense because of the high altitude.

If you are going to the Kruger National Park from Johannesburg, which is a high-risk malarial region, you must consider malaria prophylactics. These can be obtained from SAA Netcare Travel Clinics within South Africa, and there are several branches in Johannesburg (www.travelclinic.co.za).

Alternatively, if you wish to be prepared and already intend to visit the Kruger or Transvaal regions, visit your doctor or a recommended travel clinic before travelling. Currently there are three malaria tablets which are effective for this region: Lariam (mefloquine), doxycycline and Malarone. These tablets are available on prescription only in the UK because they may not suit everyone. Seek professional help to select the one most appropriate for your trip. As well as taking malaria prophylaxis you should also remember to apply a good insect repellent containing the chemical DEET (eg: Repel), especially between dusk and dawn when malaria mosquitoes are airborne, and to cover your arms and legs with clothing. If entering a risk area, remember to check for fevers anything from seven days into your trip and up to a year after, though the first three months is most likely. Any fever of 38°C or above should make you go to a doctor and check for malaria. This disease is treatable as long as you seek advice as soon as possible.

TRAVEL CLINICS AND HEALTH INFORMATION A full list of current travel clinic websites worldwide is available from the International Society of Travel Medicine at www.istm.org. For other journey preparation information, consult www.tripprep.com. Information about various medications may be found at www.emedicine.com. For information on malaria prevention, see www.preventingmalaria.info.

UK

Hospital for Tropical Diseases Travel Clinic Mortimer Market Building, Capper St (off Tottenham Ct Rd), London WC1E 6AU; ☎ 020 7388 9600; www.thehtd.org. Offers consultations and advice, and is able to provide all necessary drugs and vaccines for travellers. Runs a healthline (0906 133 7733) for country-specific information and health hazards. Also stocks nets, water purification equipment and personal protection measures.

Dr Jane Wilson-Howarth

Long-haul air travel increases the risk of deep vein thrombosis. Studies have shown that flights of over five-and-a-half-hours are significant, and that people who take lots of shorter flights over a short space of time may also form clots. People at highest risk are: those who have had a clot before – unless they are now taking warfarin; people over 80 years of age; anyone who has recently undergone a major operation, or surgery for varicose veins; someone who has had a hip or knee replacement in the last three months; cancer sufferers; those who have ever had a stroke; people with heart disease and those with a close blood relative who has had a clot.

Those with a slightly increased risk are people over 40; women who are pregnant or have had a baby in the last couple of weeks; people taking female hormones, the contraceptive pill or other oestrogen therapy; heavy smokers; those who have very severe varicose veins; the very obese and people who are very tall (over 6ft/1.8m) or short (under 5ft/1.5m).

A deep vein thrombosis (DVT) is a blood clot that forms in the deep leg veins. This is very different from irritating but harmless superficial phlebitis. DVT causes swelling and redness of one leg, usually with heat and pain in one calf and sometimes the thigh. A DVT is only dangerous if a clot breaks away and travels to the lungs (pulmonary embolus). Symptoms of a pulmonary embolus (PE) include chest pain that is worse on breathing in deeply, shortness of breath, and sometimes coughing up small amounts of blood. The symptoms commonly start three to ten days after a long flight. Anyone who thinks that they might have a DVT needs to see a doctor immediately who will arrange a scan.

PREVENTION OF DVT Several conditions make the problem more likely. Immobility is the key, and factors including reduced oxygen in cabin air and dehydration may also contribute. To reduce the risk of thrombosis on a long journey:

- Exercise before and after the flight
- Keep mobile during the flight; move around every couple of hours
- Drink plenty of non-fizzy water or juices during the flight
- Avoid taking sleeping pills and excessive alcohol
- Perform exercises that mimic walking and tense the calf muscles
- Consider wearing flight socks or support stockings (see www.legshealth.com)
- Take a meal of oily fish (mackerel, trout, salmon, sardines, etc) in the 24 hours before departure to reduce blood clotability and thus DVT risk

If you think you are at increased risk of a clot, ask your doctor if it is safe to travel.

MASTA (Medical Advisory Service for Travellers Abroad) MASTA Ltd, Moorfield Rd, Yeadon LS19 7BN; ☎ 0870 606 2782; www.masta-travel-health.com. Provides travel health advice, anti-malarials and vaccinations. There are over 25 MASTA pre-travel clinics in Britain; call or check online for the nearest. Clinics also sell mosquito nets, medical kits, insect protection and travel hygiene products.

Nomad Travel Store/Clinic 3–4 Wellington Terrace, Turnpike Lane, London N8 0PX; ☎ 020 8889 7014; travel-healthline (office hours only) 0906 863 3414; e sales@nomadtravel.co.uk; www.nomadtravel.co.uk. Also at 40 Bernard St, London WC1N 1LJ; ☎ 020 7833 4114; 52 Grosvenor Gardens, London SW1W 0AG; ☎ 020 7823 5823; and 43 Queens Rd, Bristol BS8 1QH; ☎ 0117 922 6567. For health advice, equipment such as mosquito nets and other anti-bug devices, and an excellent range of adventure travel gear.

Trailfinders Travel Clinic 194 Kensington High St, London W8 7RG; ☎ 020 7938 3999; www.trailfinders.com/clinic.htm. Doctor-led travel clinic with free consultation. No appointment needed. Open Mon–Sat. Up-to-date advice and vaccines, and all currently used malaria tablets are available. Also a good range of travel guides and other travel goods sold.

USA

Centers for Disease Control 1600 Clifton Rd, Atlanta, GA 30333; ☎ 800 311 3435; travellers' health hotline ☎ 888 232 3299; www.cdc.gov/travel. The central source of travel information in the US. The invaluable *Health Information for International Travel*, published annually, is available from the Division of Quarantine at this address.

IAMAT (International Association for Medical Assistance to Travelers) 1623 Military Rd, 279, Niagara Falls, NY14304-1745; ☎ 716 754 4883; e info@iamat.org; www.iamat.org. A non-profit organisation that provides lists of English-speaking doctors abroad.

SAFETY

In the 1980s and 1990s Johannesburg was frequently dubbed the most dangerous city in the world, although crime rates have declined considerably. To reduce paranoia, remember that much of the serious, violent crime is gang-based and occurs in areas that tourists are unlikely to visit such as Hillbrow. Although it's feasible to drive yourself to Soweto as long as you stick to the tourist areas, it's still best to visit here and other townships such as Alexandra on a guided tour; anyway, you will miss out without a guide. The Newtown precinct in the city centre is safe to visit and security is good. However, the rest of the city centre for now is still best to visit on a city tour, and never go to Hillbrow unless you are accompanied. The suburbs are regarded as considerably safer than the inner city though there are isolated incidents.

Dangers facing visitors are generally limited to theft, mugging or, on occasion, car jacking, and these can be avoided by taking common sense precautions such as keeping an eye on who's around you, avoiding trouble spots, not walking or driving around at night, and not flashing your valuables. If driving around Johannesburg even in the day, get local advice on your route to ensure you don't end up in a dodgy part of town and keep windows and doors locked. Carry a street map; Johannesburg is a large city and it's easy to get lost. Never stop for accidents or for another motorist who has broken down. This could be a scam to get you out of your car. Never leave anything on show in your car and always make use of car guards (see *Tipping*, below). The city produces a leaflet, *Safety Tips for Tourists*, that is available around the city at

NOTES FOR DISABLED TRAVELLERS

Gordon Rattray (www.able-travel.com)

AIRPORTS OR Tambo International Airport has well trained staff, is fully equipped and is as efficient as any European counterpart. Smaller domestic airports may not be as reliable.

ACCOMMODATION Most quality hotels in and around the city contain some adapted rooms. However, the more budget conscious you are, the more limited your options will be. To be sure you get what you need, good research must be done in advance.

GETTING AROUND Modern shopping malls are designed with disabled people in mind and many restaurants, museums, theatres and other attractions are accessible, at least to some degree. Again, it is essential to check in advance. The city's pavements and streets are not sufficiently adapted to make wheeling easy, and taxis, buses and trains are also not wheelchair accessible. Therefore, if you cannot transfer independently, it's advisable to contact the specialist operators (see below) who run adapted vehicles.

Cars with paraplegic hand controls can be hired from **Avis Car Rental** (✆ +27 (0)11 923 3660; e *reservations@avis.co.za; www.avis.co.za*) and **Hertz** (✆ +27 (0)21 935 4800; e *res@hertz.co.za; www.hertz.co.za*).

HEALTH Although South African healthcare is of a high standard, it is essential to understand and to be able to explain your own medical requirements. Take all necessary medication and equipment packed in your hand luggage in case your main luggage gets lost.

SECURITY As a disabled person, you are more vulnerable than most tourists. Stay aware of where your belongings are, especially during car transfers and similar activities where the confusion creates easy pickings for an opportunist thief.

SPECIALIST OPERATORS The following operators cater for disabled clients, and can provide advice and transport as well as organise city tours and safaris further afield:

Bophelo Tours & Safaris \ +27 (0)12 654 9189; f +27 (0)12 654 7237; e marius@bophelo.com; www.bophelo.com

Endeavour Safaris \/f +27 (0)21 556 6114; e info@endeavour-safaris.com; www.endeavour-safaris.com

Epic Enabled \/f +27 (0)21 782 9575; e info@epic-enabled.com; www.epic-enabled.com

Titch Tours \ +27 (0)21 686 5501; f +27 21 686 5506; e titcheve@iafrica.com; www.titchtours.co.za

FURTHER INFORMATION The *Access Gauteng* guide is a highly rated booklet, which gives details of accessible accommodation, attractions and tour operators in the region, plus information about other topics such as wheelchair hire. You can order a copy from the Gauteng Tourist Authority (*PO Box 155, Newtown 2113, Johannesburg;* \ +27 (0)11 832 2780/639 1600; e *tourism@gauteng.net; www.gauteng.net*)

The Quad/Para Association of South Africa (\ +27 (0)31 767 0348; f +27 (0)31 767 0584; e *ari@qasa.co.za; www.qasa.co.za*) provides advice about all mobility issues.

tourist venues such as hotels and can also be downloaded in PDF format from www.joburg.org.za/tourists/crimetips1.pdf.

For women, travel in South Africa carries the same usual rules as in most big cities, of being cautious at night, not going to deserted areas alone, never hitchhiking and not accepting drinks from strangers. The rape statistics in South Africa are

HEALTH AND BEAUTY JO'BURG STYLE

Given that most people in the northern suburbs lead affluent lifestyles, Johannesburg has dozens of health and beauty spas – even Soweto has one. Although perhaps not your typical Afrikaner type *oke* (bloke), many modern Johannesburg men as well as women spend a great deal of time and money on their appearance. Costs of beauty and wellness treatments are considerably lower than in, say, Europe, and as well as standard massages and facials, hot stone therapies, hydrotherapy, seaweed wraps and sea salt scrubs are some of the other toe-curling treatments on offer. There are plenty of day or half-day packages to choose from, many of them designed for couples. Some include meals and transport. If you are on a long evening flight out of Johannesburg, but have to book out of your hotel in the morning, visit a spa for a few hours of pampering before going to the airport. This will certainly make a long flight much more relaxing. Check out *www.healthspas.co.za,* which has information on all of Johannesburg's spas, and you can make reservations online. There are also spas at the big hotels such as the Westcliffe, Park alarming and are some of the highest in the world. Though it is largely a domestic problem, there have been isolated incidents against female tourists. If you are unfamiliar with the terrain don't drive alone and at the very least carry a mobile phone. At night always lock hotel doors. Overall, it is a chauvinistic culture as compared to western Europe.

Hyatt, Hilton and the Emperors Palace Casino. The latter even offers a chocolate mousse body wrap!

Plastic surgery and cosmetic dentistry are also very popular in South Africa, and the 'surgery and safari' type of holiday is increasingly being offered to foreigners. It's estimated that plastic surgery costs two thirds to a half of what it costs in the US or Europe, and the quality of the cutting edge technology and the reputation of South Africa's surgeons and dentists is amongst the best in the world. It's not just about cosmetic procedures either; burns and scar victims make their way to South Africa from overseas to get specialised laser treatment, and many people on holiday have their eyesight corrected whilst they are there – it costs about half the price to get your eyes zapped by lasers in South Africa than it does in the UK. There are several tour operators that offer these packages; tap 'surgery and safari' into Google, or get information from the Association of Plastic and Reconstruction Surgery of South Africa (APRSSA) (www.plasticsurgeons.co.za).

EMERGENCY TELEPHONE NUMBERS

AA Roadside Rescue Emergencies ☏ 083 84322
Ambulance ☏ 10177
Jo'burg Emergency Connect ☏ 011 375 5911; equipped to find any emergency number you need
Metro Emergency Rescue Service ☏ 10177

MTN emergency ☏ 112; 24-hr medical services and ambulance
Netcare ☏ 0800 002 609
SA Police Emergency ☏ 10111
Vodacom emergency ☏ 147

WHAT TO TAKE

There are very few items that cannot be bought in South Africa, often more cheaply than at home so, apart from the essentials like passport etc, you do not need to stress about forgetting anything. Indeed, Johannesburg has some fine shopping malls, so ensure you have plenty of space in your luggage to shop up a storm, and remember that tourists can claim VAT refunds on their purchases (see below). South Africa uses 220V three round pin plugs and you will need an adapter. These can be found at the airports or are widely available in South African hardware shops.

$ MONEY

CURRENCY Exchange rates at the time of going to press were £1 = R13.99; US$1 = R7.33; €1 = R9.37. For the latest exchange rates, go to www.xe.com. The South African currency is the rand (R). Notes are in R200, R100, R50, R20 and R10; coins are R5, R2, R1, R0.50, R0.20, R0.10 and R0.05. The rand is a strong currency and can also be used interchangeably in the neighbouring countries of Swaziland, Lesotho, Mozambique and Namibia and is accepted for purchases and to pay for the likes of hotel rooms in Mozambique to the south of Beira.

BUDGETING Whilst not as cheap as it once was, South Africa is still good value by European standards. At the bottom backpacker end, expect to pay around R80–100 for a bed in a dorm, which will include bedding, so you do not need a sleeping bag. Costs can be kept down by making your own breakfast, buying sandwiches or salads from a supermarket and budgeting perhaps R100 for dinner and a few drinks in a chain restaurant or cheaper café/bar. Mid-range travellers staying in guesthouses or the chain hotels would be looking at paying R500–900 per night per couple for a double room, slightly less for a single, which would include all mod cons such as en suite bathroom and TV. There are plenty of top-of-the-range hotels in Johannesburg which have the stamp of luxury, which cost upwards of R1,000–1,500 a night for a double. A two-course meal in a reasonable restaurant with wine will cost around R150 per person. For special treats there are also a number of fabulous restaurants around the city, many serving gourmet food with extensive wine lists, but even these are not too expensive at around R35 for a starter or dessert and R75–100 for a main course, slightly more for seafood, and a bottle of wine for R70–100. To get the price of a meal down, check with the restaurant when booking a table if they offer corkage; many charge a fee of R20–30 corkage and you bring your own wine which can be bought at supermarkets from only R20 a bottle. If you are hiring a car, budget on R200–350 per day depending on the class of the car. Petrol costs about two thirds of what it does in Europe.

TIPPING Tipping in restaurants is expected: a 10% tip is about right for good service. Tipping hotel staff is optional and not expected, though a few rand to a hotel porter for carrying your luggage is only polite. If you go on a day tour and you've had an informative and interesting time then tipping the tour guide will be much appreciated. It is customary in South Africa to tip car guards. They usually wear a work vest or badge and for R2–5 will watch over your car while you are away. This system is worth supporting as it provides thousands of jobs. In petrol stations attendants fill up the car, take payment, wash the windscreen and check oil and water if desired. For this a tip of R2–5 is usual.

VAT REFUNDS Tourists to South Africa can reclaim the 14% VAT back on purchases bought in the country on anything over R250. To reach the R250 you can combine smaller purchases so it doesn't have to be a single item. Reclaims can be done at the airport and the border posts, and the process is reasonably efficient, though do allow yourself extra time before your flight. Items purchased must be shown to the customs officer with the corresponding VAT receipts, which get stamped. Most shops these days print their VAT number on receipts, but double check when you are buying something. At the airport this needs to be done before you check in your luggage so you can repack items, and the desk is in the departures hall where you check in. The officer hands you back the stamped receipts, you can repack and check in, and then once through into the departures lounge take your receipts to one of the two VAT Refund offices; there's one at each end of international departures. Here you are issued with a cheque for the refund which you can cash in at the bureaux de change next door for rand. You then have the choice of spending the rand at the airport or swapping it into your own currency. In theory refunds only apply to unused goods taken out of the country so try and keep labels, price tags, packaging etc with your purchase.

If you are shopping in Sandton City mall, there is a VAT refund desk here where you can immediately get your receipts stamped against goods without having to do it at the airport. You will need to present your passport and air ticket, and this desk can't give refunds, so you will still have to hand in your receipts at the airport. For more information visit www.taxrefunds.co.za.

3 Practicalities

$ BANKS AND MONEY MATTERS

It is of course a matter of personal preference how you carry your money; cash, travellers' cheques or debit and credit cards are all OK, and all banks have foreign exchange facilities. It's perfectly feasible to get by on credit and debit cards only, as there are ATMs at all the banks, shopping malls and most petrol stations. Visa, MasterCard, American Express and Diners are all honoured by most establishments. Cards usually give the best exchange rates, though remember your bank at home will charge a small fee for withdrawing from an ATM abroad. The amount you can withdraw varies between systems and cards, but you should be able to take out up to R1,000 a day. Note that the current account option on an ATM is called a cheque account in South Africa. There have been problems with ATM fraud and robbery in South Africa. Remember to never accept help from a stranger at an ATM, ensure no-one is looking over your shoulder, and use an ATM in a secure place such as a shopping mall or one that has a security guard on duty. If you are hiring a car it is essential to have a credit card (not a debit card). The chip and pin system has recently been introduced and is catching on in shops and restaurants. The only thing you can't pay for with a card is petrol, which is cash only. It's a good idea to send yourself an email to a secure site with credit card numbers and the customer service telephone numbers. In the event of a stolen card, phone

American Express ☏ 011 359 0200
Diners Club ☏ 011 358 8406
MasterCard ☏ 0800 990 418
Visa Card ☏ 0800 990 475

Banking hours are Monday–Friday 09.00–15.30, Saturday 09.00–11.00. In shopping malls, banks with foreign exchange facilities stay open until 19.00 and at the airport exchange facilities are open to accommodate all flight arrivals. Apart from the banks there are branches of American Express (☏ *011 467 8140; www.americanexpress.co.za)* and Rennies Travel (*Thomas Cook agent,* ☏ *011 884 4025; www.rennies.co.za)* in the shopping malls. Phone for the nearest branch.

☏ COMMUNICATIONS

INTERNET Note that the connection on the end of a telephone jack in South Africa is different to the UK, so if you are plugging in your own laptop to a telephone line you will have to get a different cable available from computer and telephone shops in South Africa. There are three internet cafés at the airport where you can also plug in your own laptop, and wireless is available throughout the shopping and dining areas. Elsewhere wireless is catching on fast: there are over 200 wireless hotspots in Johannesburg and this figure is growing daily. These are mostly in hotel lobbies, some cafés and restaurants, and some of the shopping malls. Most of the major hotels have business centres, and if they have wireless offer top-up cards for sale at reception. Regular dial-up internet is available from most hotel rooms, and in the smaller guesthouses and backpackers, at least one computer is available for guests' use. All the shopping malls have internet cafés and internet access is also available at most branches of *Postnet* (a print and stationery shop) and *Vodacom* (mobile phone shops).

POST Post offices are efficient but I have my doubts about the South African postal service as I have had things go missing in the past. Post anything of any value by registered post that you can track, or use a courier service. Post offices can be found in all the shopping malls and are generally open Monday–Friday 09.00–16.30, and Saturday 09.00–12.00. Surface mail to Europe takes about six weeks, whilst a letter by airmail shouldn't take more than a week. If you want to send something quickly, go to the post office at the airport, where for a small extra fee, letters will go on the next flight. All post offices accept credit cards. For the nearest branch ↘ 0860 111 502 or visit www.sapo.co.za.

Postal rates To send a letter or postcard from South Africa to the UK or the US costs around R4.40. Phonecards come in denominations of R20, R50 and R100.

TELEPHONE There are card and coin phones throughout the city, from which you can dial direct to anywhere in the world. Phonecards are available from supermarkets and small shops. Phoning from hotel rooms is considerably more expensive.

If you are using your mobile phone, you need to ascertain which local networks have roaming agreements with your country network; visit the three mobile phone providers at www.mtn.co.za, www.vodacom.co.za and www.cellc.co.za. If you don't want to use roaming on your mobile, then SIM cards are available from phone shops or supermarkets; a start-up pack costs around R100. Mobile phones, wireless internet and pre-paid cards can be rented from Johannesburg airport and many of the car-hire companies provide phones on a pay-as-you-go system. Note that mobile-phone chargers in South Africa have two-pin plugs so you will need to bring an adapter if you're bringing a charger from home.

Useful telephone numbers and codes

Country code	☏ 027	International operator	☏ 0009
International access code	☏ 09	International enquiries	☏ 1025
Directory enquiries	☏ 1023		

MEDIA

PRESS *The Sunday Times* and *Sunday Independent* are weekly English-language papers with national coverage, although an edition is specifically published for Johannesburg.

The excellent weekly *Mail & Guardian* is fairly high-brow and similar to the *Guardian* in the UK. Daily English-language newspapers include *The Star, Business Day, The Citizen* and *The Sowetan,* and the weekly *City Press*. One- to two-day-old European and US newspapers are available from branches of Exclusive Books (see page 133),

GIVING SOMETHING BACK

Nkosi Johnson was one of Johannesburg's most special little boys. He was born HIV-positive in a township east of Johannesburg in 1989, and whilst he was a statistic (one of more than 70,000 children are born HIV-positive every year in South Africa), he was a fighter, and at the time was the longest surviving child to be born with full blown AIDS. Nkosi died at the age of 12 on International Children's Day in 2001. When he was two, he was adopted by a volunteer worker, Gail Johnson, and moved in to her upmarket home in Melville. His mother died of an AIDS-related illness in 1997. In the same year Gail tried to enrol him into a Melville primary school, but there was opposition from other parents because of his HIV-positive status. Johnson went to court and won her case and Nkosi was permitted to attend the school. The case resulted in education departments across South Africa drawing up new policies on accepting HIV/AIDS pupils (and teachers) without discrimination. Nkosi's big moment came in July 2000 when he addressed delegates at the International AIDS Conference in Durban. A tiny 11-year-old figure, with enormous eyes and wearing an oversized dark suit, nervously held his microphone, and made an emotional speech he wrote himself about his birth and life. The which also sells a wide variety of home-grown and foreign magazines. The ones specifically useful for visitors include the annually published *Eat Out* magazine, which reviews some of the better restaurants in the country; *Getaway*, which is aimed at adventurous domestic tourists but has some interesting travel articles; and *Africa*

audience of 10,000 delegates were both rapt and tearful and his performance went on to be broadcast to millions of people around the world. With childlike simplicity he asked 'Please help people with AIDS – support them, love them, care for them'. He also asked that AZT drugs be given to pregnant HIV-positive women in South Africa. Nkosi's efforts did much to acknowledge that those living with AIDS must be treated with humanity and Nelson Mandela described him as an icon of the struggle for life. South Africa has the highest number of people living with AIDS in the world and at least one out of every ten South Africans is HIV-positive. The pandemic has hit the populous black communities the most, and there are an estimated 75,000 AIDS orphans in Gauteng Province alone. In 1999 Gail opened the first Nkosi's Haven in Johannesburg's suburb of Berea, an AIDS care centre founded and named after Nkosi, and today she runs several projects caring for HIV-positive mothers and children, all of which rely on donations. If you would like to support these worthwhile causes, contact the Nkosi Johnson AIDS Foundation (*www.nkosishaven.co.za*).

Geographic, which covers wildlife and the environment with superb glossy photographs.

RADIO The South African Broadcast Corporation (SABC) has numerous national stations catering for the 11 official languages. *5FM* is the SABC national pop music station, while *Metro FM* offers R 'n' B, hip-hop and kwaito. Other popular pop stations are *Highveld FM* and *Kaya FM* in Johannesburg and *Jacaranda FM* in Pretoria.

TELEVISION Again the SABC produces a number of programmes in English, followed by Afrikaans, Zulu and Xhosa broadcast on SABC 1, 2 and 3. South African television is not brilliant, however, and forget about daytime TV unless you're into the *Bold and the Beautiful* and other rubbishy soaps from the US. The fourth free channel, etv, is better and has a few foreign imports. The paying channel, M-Net, has the better South African TV as well as sport and Hollywood movies. DSTV, with a range of channels from MTV to BBC Prime, is found in most hotels.

❺ EMBASSIES & CONSULATES

There are scores of embassies in Pretoria, some with consulates in Johannesburg (though for passport-related enquiries, you will have to go to Pretoria). There are far too many to list but visit www.joburg.org.za/tourists/consulates1.stm for full details.

4 Local Transport

✈ AIR

There is an extensive and efficient domestic air service with regular daily flights connecting Johannesburg with the other major cities in South Africa, all of which can be reached on flights of no longer than two hours. They also fly to regional cities such as Harare, Victoria Falls, Lusaka, Windhoek and Maputo. On popular routes such as Johannesburg to Cape Town or Durban, the cost of a ticket is usually only a little more expensive than a bus ticket. Good deals can be found if you book early online, especially through the no-frills airlines.

British Airways/Comair ✆ 011 921 0222; www.britishairways.com. BA's southern African operator, Comair links South Africa's larger cities and the regional hubs.

Kulula ✆ 0861 585 852; www.kulula.com. Also owned by British Airways, Kulula is a no-frills airline and fun to fly with. The crew wear jeans and T-shirts, and you are reminded not to forget your husband when you leave the plane. Regular daily flights between the cities, and services to Harare and Windhoek on a code share basis with BA.

Nationwide ✆ 0861 737 737; www.flynationwide.co.za. Regional flights plus a daily service between Johannesburg and Gatwick in the UK.

One Time ☎ 0861 345345; www.1time.co.za. Another good value, no-frills airline with nice leather-seated planes, but not as extensive a network of routes as Kulula.

South African Airways ☎ 011 978 1111; www.flysaa.com. Flights all round the country, as well as other southern African cities in conjunction with both SA Airlink and SA Express.

AIRPORT SHUTTLES

OR Tambo International Airport is about a 30-minute drive from the city centre and about 40 minutes from the northern suburbs. All accommodation options can pre-arrange a shuttle transfer, so ask about this when making a room reservation. You will need rand to pay the driver, so if you haven't already got some, change money at the airport. Expect to pay in the region of R200–250 depending on how far you're going; the price comes down the more people are in the van. Taxis are available at the airport but shuttles are much cheaper. Most international flights arrive early in the morning and depart in the evening, and given that these are also the busiest times for commuter traffic, it's a good idea to pre-book a shuttle. However, if you haven't, the shuttle companies have desks in the arrivals hall of the airport and in the Parkade Centre opposite the domestic terminal.

Airport Link ☎ 011 884 3957
Impala Bus Shuttle ☎ 011 975 0510
Johannesburg Airport Shuttle ☎ 011 394 6902
Magic Bus ☎ 011 548 0822; www.magicbus.co.za

BUSES

Metro buses run seven days a week between 06.00 and 19.00 and mostly serve the city's commuters. Buses generally run between the bus station in Ghandhi (formerly Vanderbiji) Square in the city centre and the northern suburbs along Jan Smuts Avenue, Oxford, Louis Botha and Barry Hertzog roads, though there are over 100 bus routes in the city. They have recently acquired a new fleet of smart double-decker buses. Tickets cost R2–7 depending on how many 'zones' you cross, and a book of pre-paid tickets, available from Computicket kiosks in the shopping malls, works out cheaper than paying individual fares. Fares and timetables are on the website, or pick up a timetable at Ghandhi Square.

Metro Bus ☎ 011 838 2125; www.mbus.co.za

CAR HIRE

Johannesburg is easy enough to get around by car, though Jo'burgers are known for their fast driving and at peak commuter times traffic can be heavy. The city is surrounded by a tangle of multi-lane highways, and it's a big city so you'll need a good road map (available from bookshops and petrol stations) and be aware of the suburbs where it is not advised to casually drive through. There is a danger of car jacking so be wary at night, stick to the main roads, and keep doors locked and windows up. If you stop at traffic lights (known as 'robots' in South Africa) or four-way stops and spot anything suspicious, check for crossing traffic and just drive through. The numbers of the international car hire companies are free phone within South Africa; for overseas reservations go through the websites. Compare rates or contact two or three local companies listed under 'car and camper hire' at South African Yellow Pages (✆ *086 093 5569; www.yellowpages.co.za*). You can also hire a car instantly on arrival at the airport, and the hotels and backpackers will be able to arrange a car for you within an hour or two. You'll need a valid driver's licence, a credit card and your passport. It's a legal requirement to wear a seat belt and the speed limit is 120km/h on highways and 60km/h in urban areas. Parking is available just about everywhere, but remember if you are parking on a street it is best to find somewhere with a car guard who should be tipped to watch over your car (see page 52).

Avis ✆ 0861 021 111; www.avis.co.za
Budget ✆ 0861 016 622; www.budget.co.za
Hertz ✆ 0861 600 136; www.hertz.co.za
Imperial ✆ 0861 131 000; www.imperialcarrental.co.za
Tempest/Sixt ✆ 0806 031 666; www.tempestcarhire.co.za
Aroundabout Cars ✆ 0860 422 4022; www.aroundaboutcars.com. This is a recommended national agent that can offer competitive rates from the local car-hire companies.

IN AND OUT OF JO'BURG

The N1 runs through the entire country from the Zimbabwean border to Cape Town via Johannesburg and Pretoria. From Jo'burg it's approximately 1,400km to Cape Town through the Great Karoo, and most people choose to break the journey with an overnight stay at either Bloemfontein, roughly one third of the way, or Beaufort West, two thirds of the way, where there are numerous accommodation options for motorists. The N3 heads south to Durban which is approximately 570km or 5½-hr drive away, and most people stop in Harrismith, which is roughly half-way, for refreshments and to stretch their legs at one of the very many service stations. Both the N1 and N3 are very busy in December when Gauteng families bound for the Cape or the seaside resorts on the KwaZulu coast go on their long Christmas holidays. The N7 runs from east to west and links Johannesburg and Pretoria with both Gaborone in Botswana and Maputo in Mozambique. All of these roads have toll booths placed every few kilometres, and although tolls vary on each route, expect to pay around R0.25 per kilometre.

For those starting a longer trip of southern Africa in Johannesburg, there are also a number of companies that rent out fully equipped 4x4 vehicles or camper vans for camping holidays (though there is nowhere to camp in Johannesburg itself).

Britz 011 396 1860; www.britz.co.za
Bushlore Africa 011 792 5300; www.bushlore.com
Kea Campers 011 397 2435; www.keacampers.co.za
Maui Camper Hire 011 396 1445; www.maui.co.za

METRO COMMUTER TRAINS

Johannesburg has a network of metro commuter services linking the suburbs to the business districts. These should generally be avoided as there have been many cases of robbery, and a white face on these is a rare sight indeed. However, safety and security is tightening up in the city, so the train network may be a viable option in the future. In New York City a few years ago, the subway was considered dangerous, but today it's used by everyone and is considered a safe and comfortable way to travel. Let's hope that this happens in Johannesburg.

MINIBUS TAXIS

These generally run between the townships, the city and the suburbs taking people to and from work. They are generally unmarked, white 12-seater minibuses and there are no formal stops. They are simply waved down from the side of the road and commuters and drivers have a special sign language to determine where the taxi is heading. For example, by cupping hands into an O shape, the passenger on

THE GAUTRAIN

The Gautrain Rapid Rail Link is presently being built and is scheduled to be up and running by the 2010 Football World Cup (indeed it was part of the conditions of granting the city the World Cup). Although in recent years it hasn't all been plain railing financially speaking, in the 2006 budget, Finance Minister Trevor Manuel set aside R7 billion for the project. It will comprise two links, between Pretoria and Johannesburg, and OR Tambo International Airport and Sandton. Altogether there will be about 80km of rail, with three major stations at Pretoria, Johannesburg and the airport, as well as stations at Rosebank, Sandton, Marlboro, Midrand, Centurion, Hatfield and Kempton Park. The train will travel at a maximum speed of 160km/h and the journey between Johannesburg and Pretoria will be about 40 minutes with stops, whilst the journey from the airport to Sandton will be about 15 minutes. There is talk about developing an airline check-in facility at Sandton Station. The N1 highway between Pretoria and Johannesburg carries an astonishing 300,000 vehicles a day on weekdays, so if commuters make the switch from car to train, traffic congestion and pollution would decrease significantly. Check out www.gautrain.co.za for progress.

the side of the road is indicating that he wants to go to Orlando. If the taxi is going to Orlando then it will stop. They are not really recommended for visitors as they are driven rather recklessly, you will have no idea where the taxi is going to, petty theft is a problem at the taxi ranks (where the taxis start and finish their journeys), and most seats are booked by commuters. However, there's no reason why you can't jump on one (if there's space) for a short hop up the road. They cost about R1 per kilometre. Recent legislation to get un-roadworthy vehicles off the roads and proper licensing into place is underway, so this form of transport should improve considerably over the next few years. They are also known as *Zola Budds* in Johannesburg, after the famous Olympic South African runner.

TAXIS

Taxis cannot be hailed in the street so you'll have to order one. All are metered, and expect to pay around R40 for a journey of about three kilometres. This is actually quite expensive compared to other places in the world, but a tip for large groups (which brings the price down considerably) is to ask the company if they can send a Venture; these carry nine passengers. Any hotel and restaurant can phone a taxi for you and they materialise pretty quickly.

Corporate Cabs ✆ 0800 800 800; www.corporatecabs.co.za

LOCAL TOUR OPERATORS

To get the most out of the sights, especially the historical ones, it's best to go on a tour with an informative guide. Most use minibuses, have registered drivers and guides, and will pick up at all hotels. On the township tours most guides are township residents and can really share an insight about the history and make-up of the townships. Tourism to the townships has created very many jobs, raises income that goes back into the townships, and is a real highlight to a trip to South Africa – in fact, figures show that these days more visitors go to Soweto than Kruger National Park. All of the following operators offer half-day tours to Soweto, which usually include visits to the suburbs of Orlando, Diepkloof, Dube and Pimville, with stops to see the former homes of Nelson Mandela and Desmond Tutu, Walter Sisulu Square of Independence, Regina Mundi Cathedral, Hector Peterson Memorial and an informal settlement. The operators can also organise night-time tours to the *shebeens*. Other tours on offer include trips to the historical township of Alexandra, Gold Reef City, city centre tours, Lion Park, Lesedi Village and Sterkfontein Caves. Discuss with the tour operator what you would like to do. This is a far from comprehensive list of tour operators. Your hotel or hostel can also recommend an operator, or contact the tourist office. Expect to pay in the region of R250–300 for a half-day tour.

Gold Reef Guides ☏ 011 496 1400; www.goldreefguides.co.za. Specialises in Gold Reef City as the name suggests, but also runs township tours and can arrange helicopter flights over Soweto.
Jimmy's Face to Face Tours ☏ 011 331 6109; www.face2face.co.za. The original Soweto tour company that has taken thousands of people since 1985. Also offers a 5-hr evening tour to Soweto for dinner and jazz, plus city centre tours and Gold Reef City tours.

JMT Tours ✎ 011 980 6038; www.jmtours.co.za. Run by Joe Motsogi, who was involved in the 1976 Soweto Uprising. Goes to Soweto, Lesedi Village, Gold Reef City, amongst other places.

Karabo Tours ✎ 011 325 7125; www.backpackers-ritz.co.za. Full range of affordable tours, to Soweto and Lion Park, plus a full-day Pretoria city tour; based at the Backpackers Ritz but will pick up from all northern suburb hotels.

Lords Travel & Tours ✎ 011 791 5494; www.lordstravel.co.za. Day tours plus longer trips to Sun City and Kruger.

Moratiwa Tours ✎ 011 869 6629; www.moratiwatours.co.za. Soweto tours including an overnight one, and a variety of tours all around Johannesburg and Pretoria.

Pulse Africa ✎ 011 325 2290; www.pulseafrica.com

The Rock Soweto ✎ 011 986 8182; e tebogo@therock.co.za. Tours of Soweto and Gold Reef City.

TK Tours ✎ 011 869 6390; www.tktours.co.za. All local day tours plus Cradle of Humankind and Pretoria city tours and visits to the Cullinan Mine.

Vhupi Cruiseliner Tours ✎ 011 936 0411; www.vhupo-tours.com. Selection of Soweto, Alexandra and city centre tours, including nightlife tours.

5 Accommodation

With an estimated 32,000 hotel beds, there is no shortage of accommodation in Johannesburg. Most establishments are located in the northern suburbs or are clustered around the airport, and these days there are few options in the city centre itself suitable for visitors – though this may change with the tide of investment. It would certainly be nice to see some of the historical buildings in the city centre being turned into boutique hotels. Most hotels are geared for the business traveller, and as such there are a variety of chains of modern anonymous blocks that are perfectly functional and comfortable, but hardly need a separate listing as each room is identical whether you are staying in Bryanston or Sandton. I have dealt with the chains separately below. Unfortunately, of the other individual hotels, not many stand out for their character or charm, and again most are modern and have been built within the last couple of decades as the northern suburbs developed. Nevertheless, the advantage of this is that the standards are high, with all the mod cons you'd expect of a modern hotel room, and service is generally very good. There are also some award-winning top-class hotels at the luxury end of the market which are on a par with the rest of the world's five-star establishments.

Some people prefer the anonymity of a hotel, but for those that don't there are a few good guesthouses and B&Bs with just a few rooms where you are likely to become friendly with the hosts. Township B&Bs are also springing up and it's a worthwhile experience to stay the night with a local family. There are a couple of good backpackers' hostels and these represent the cheapest accommodation in the city. Remember they also have double rooms so it's not just a case of sleeping in a dorm with a load of strangers.

Accommodation in South Africa is monitored by the Tourism Grading Council of South Africa (TGCSA). All tourist accommodation is graded annually by inspectors, for its overall standard of furnishings, comfort, guest care, service and functionality, and is awarded a star grading. You can pick up a copy of the TGCSA's *Accommodation Guide* in bookshops or visit the website for more information (*www.tourismgrading.co.za*).

Rates listed are to be used as a guide and are based on two people sharing a double room. All the listed establishments accept credit cards. Remember to look out for specials on the websites and bear in mind that some places offer discounts if booking online. Except at the backpackers and the City Lodge group, all rates include breakfast.

CHAIN HOTELS

THE CITY LODGE GROUP There are City Lodges, Town Lodges and Road Lodges all over Johannesburg. All are in blocks with a car park and are perfectly comfortable and functional, with made-for-hotel furniture, AC, tea- and coffee-making facilities, TV, wireless or dial-up internet, and wheelchair access. They are strategically located close to the main highways or intersections and usually have a chain restaurant close. You can book online, but if you phone and the hotel is full (which they frequently are) the receptionists will try and get you into another one nearby. If you just want to pull over, watch a movie, shower and sleep, they're absolutely fine. Except for the Courtyard Suites, breakfast is extra. The ones near the airport offer a shuttle service. What differs between each group are the facilities and the price. The largest rooms can be found at the Courtyard Suites (*www.courtyard.co.za*) and start from R750, and these hotels have a little bit more individuality than the others in the group and have their own restaurant, bar and swimming pool. The City Lodges (*www.citylodge.co.za*) have spacious rooms from R550 and extra additions such as a pool, bar and coffee shop where breakfast is served. The Town Lodges (*www.townlodge.co.za*) are the same as the City Lodges but with smaller rooms from R515, with shower only (no bath), and no pool. The Road Lodges (*www.roadlodge.co.za*) are the best value in the group and the rates are the same for 1–3 people and start from R290, though the rooms are tiny and if there is a third person sleeping on the fold-out sleeper chair there's no floor space left. The minuscule bathrooms are behind a sliding door. There's no bar, but breakfast is available, and they're modern and cheap.

GARDEN COURT (*www.southernsun.com*) These hotels used to be the Holiday Inn Garden Court, but recently they have dropped the Holiday Inn branding. Stay Easy used to be the Holiday Inn Express, a slightly cheaper version of Garden Court. The hotels are owned by Southern Sun and can all be booked online with a 5% discount. It's obviously not difficult to visualise what was once a Holiday Inn; they're all very similar, modern blocks with 100 + rooms and car parks, good service and facilities, and they all have restaurants, bars and swimming pools. *Room rates start from R850, with discounts at the weekends.*

THE DON (*www.don.co.za*) This chain of luxury apartments and suites is the only chain of hotels listed on the Stock Exchange to be wholly black-owned and managed. Depending on the hotel, there is a choice of double studios, or 1–3 bedroom suites with a spacious lounge and dining space, fully equipped kitchen, work stations for laptops, and high quality modern furnishings. If you don't want to make your own breakfast, there's also the choice of eating in the breakfast room. There's secure parking and a swimming pool at each, and rates practically halve if you stay for over a month. You can explore 3D images of the suites and make reservations on the website; online bookings attract up to a 10% discount. *Rates start from R710 for a studio, through to R1,685 for a 3-bedroom apartment.*

AIRPORT AND EAST OF THE CITY

⌂ **Africa Centre** 65 Sunny Rd, Benoni, 5min drive from the airport; ☏ 011 894 4857; www.africacentrelodge.co.za Good value friendly lodge that's used by the budget tour operators and is more like an upmarket backpackers', though there are no dorms. It's recently been extended considerably and now offers sgls, twins, dbls, group or family rooms from only R200, a helpful travel centre, internet, swimming pool, lively bar, restaurant, pool table, sauna and jacuzzi, and massages can be arranged. A good all-round option for budget travellers.

🏠 **The Airport Grand Hotel** (151 rooms, 2 for wheelchair users) 100 North Rand Rd, Boksburg, approx 10min drive along R21, opposite the East Rand Mall; ☎ 011 823 1843; www.legacyhotels.co.za
Modern brick hotel arranged around an atrium garden with swimming pool and sun loungers, 60-seater restaurant serving buffet meals, wireless internet in the lobby, pool-facing rooms, small gym and regular airport shuttles. The downside is it's right in the airport's flight path, but on the upside you can shop 'til you drop in the enormous East Rand Mall across the road. *Rates start from R790.*

🏠 **Airport Sun Inter Continental** (148 rooms) Opposite Terminal 3 at the airport; ☎ 011 961 5400;
www.southernsun.com; www.johannesburghotels.intercontinental.com
This luxury hotel is actually at the airport; the other airport hotels are 500m–3km away. It's just a 50m stroll from international arrivals across the concourse, and you can push your trolley right into your room. Flight information is displayed on TVs throughout the hotel. Facilities include a stylish ground floor bar and restaurant with lots of windows to watch the other mere plebs emerging from the airport. There's laundry, valet and baby-sitting services, a rooftop gym and beauty salon. The latter two can be used by passengers with long waits between flights. *Pricey from R2,300 per night, but you can't argue with its location, especially after a long flight.*

🏠 **D'Oreale** (196 rooms) at Emperors Palace Casino and Resort next to the airport (see page 113); 64 Jones St, Kempton Park; ☎ 011 928 1770; www.doreale.com
Absolutely over-the-top, 5-star super-luxurious casino hotel with 196 rooms decorated with sweeping drapes,

gilt, chandeliers and marble. The more expensive suites are individually decorated with antiques and pictures. Facilities include a very smart restaurant overlooking a swimming pool with a giant fountain in the middle of it, several bars, and a luxurious beauty spa with pillars, frescoes, and Roman spa bath for all sorts of treats. *Rates start from R1,790 for a classic room through to R9,570 for the presidential suite.*

🏠 **Metcourt Laurel** (56 rooms) same location as D'Oreale above; ☎ 011 928 1310; www.metcourt.com
Here there are 56 standard rooms plus some considerably more expensive suites; modern and comfortable with DSTV and safes, but very typical hotel furnishings. Guests can use the facilities at the D'Oreale and get free entry into the casino complex where there are several restaurants. I would hazard a guess that this hotel is frequented by gamblers that have stayed in the casino too late. *Rates start from R970.*

🏠 **Protea Hotel Transit** (42 rooms) Johannesburg airport; ☎ 011 390 1160; www.proteahotels.co.za.
On the 3rd floor in international departures (above the duty-free shops), and used by passengers in transit who don't actually leave the airport. *Dbls cost R859.*

🏠 **City Lodge Airport** 4 Sandvale Rd, Edenvale; ☎ 011 392 1750
🏠 **The Don Eastgate** 220 Queen St, Bruma; ☎ 011 622 2115
🏠 **The Don OR Tambo International Airport** 6 Electron Av, Isando; ☎ 011 392 6082
🏠 **Garden Court OR Tambo International Airport** 2 Hulley Rd, Kempton Park; ☎ 011 392 1062
🏠 **Road Lodge Airport** Kruin St, off Herman Rd, Germiston; ☎ 011 392 2268
🏠 **Stay Easy Eastgate** 8 South Bld, Bruma; ☎ 011 622 0060
🏠 **Town Lodge Airport** Herman Rd, Germiston; ☎ 011 974 5202

SANDTON AND AROUND

⌂ **De Kuilen Country House** (4 cottages) 30 Glenluce Dr, Douglasdale, Sandton; ☏ 011 704 2421; www.dekuilen.co.za [1 C3]

Set in three acres of countryside, this is an elegant whitewashed Cape Dutch homestead stuffed full of antiques; accommodation is in 4 cottages set within their own gardens full of roses and one delightful tree-house called Lavender Loft. Each is very private and the pretty garden terraces are wonderfully peaceful. One of the cottages has got its own kitchen and conservatory, or you can eat at the main house which also has a fine wine collection. There's also a luxury beauty spa here. *Graded as a 5-star guesthouse, rates vary amongst the cottages, but expect to pay in the region of R1,400 for a couple and R1,800 for a family.*

⌂ **Hilton Sandton** (329 rooms) 138 Rivonia Rd, Sandton; ☏ 011 322 1888; www.hilton.com [7 D2]

Within walking distance of Sandton City and Village Walk malls, this sleek modern hotel surrounded by palms spreads over 6 floors, including an upmarket executive floor. Facilities include a swimming pool, tennis court, gym, laundry/valet service, airline desk, beauty salon, and car rental desk. The Tradewinds restaurant serves extensive buffet meals. With conference facilities and a ballroom, this is a business-orientated hotel, but is nevertheless a comfortable option with international Hilton standards. *Rates are in the region of R1,650.*

⌂ **The Michelangelo** (242 rooms) Nelson Mandela Sq, Sandton; ☏ 011 883 9393; www.michelangelo.co.za; www.legacyhotels.co.za [7 C2]

This is one of the city's top hotels and a member of the Leading Hotels of the World group, and like the other 2 properties below, it commands a wonderful location on Nelson Mandela Square. Everything is arranged around a very attractive pillared atrium, and there are 242 fully equipped and elegantly decorated rooms including 2 presidential suites. Wireless internet is available in public areas and broadband in the rooms. Facilities include a special lounge facility with showers for those on early/late flights, heated indoor swimming pool, health hydro with steam bath, and several top notch restaurants. For those that want to arrive in style, VIP limousine and helicopter services are available to and from the airport. *Rates start from R2,650.*

🏠 **Michelangelo Towers** (194 rooms) 8 Maude St, Sandton; ☎ 011 245 4000; www.legacyhotels.co.za [7 C2]
The towers are the unmissable block to the south of Nelson Mandela Square and are accessed from both street level and from within the Sandton Convention Centre. The 135m tower has been around for some time, but the rooms themselves are still being fitted out — at the time of writing they had reached the 18th of the 33 floors. The views are tremendous and you can see as far as the Magaliesberg Mountains to the northwest. At the very top is a 3-storey glass penthouse with extra rooms for butlers and maids, which when completed will easily be the best and most luxurious hotel suite in Johannesburg. The 194 suites are very spacious, with wooden parquet floors and rugs, stainless steel fittings, and slate grey stylish décor with modern art on the walls. About a third of the way up the building is a complex with indoor and outdoor swimming pools, a gym, and a beauty spa with lovely fountains and tranquil treatment rooms, and in the ground floor lobby is the restaurant with very trendy décor and an expensive but expansive menu. *Room rates start from R5,300. B/fast is taken at the adjoining Michelangelo hotel.*

🏠 **Park Plaza** (138 rooms) 84 Katherine St, Sandton; ☎ 011 555 4000; www.parkplaza.com [7 D3]
This is a rather ordinary but comfortable hotel and represents excellent value, with big reductions at the w/end when rooms go for as little as R350 — not a bad price for Sandton. The other advantages are that

the ground floor rooms have motel-style parking and Sandton City is within walking distance. Ask about free pick-ups from the airport. Rooms are standard with made-for-hotel furniture and AC, and there's a restaurant, bar, terrace, gym and two swimming pools.

Protea Hotel Balalaika (330 rooms) Maude St, Sandton; ☎ 011 322 5000; www.proteahotels.co.za [7 D2] Recently refurbished to high standards in 2004, this stylish hotel is set in lovely well-established gardens with 2 swimming pools. Each of the rooms is tastefully furnished with AC and TV showing English and German satellite stations, and the suites have additional spa baths. There are 2 restaurants, one of which specialises in steak, a coffee shop and 3 bars, a gym with steam baths. The hotel is right next door to the Village Walk Mall. *Rates from R1,400.*

Raphael Penthouse Suites (60 rooms) South Tower, Nelson Mandela Sq, Sandton; ☎ 011 806 6888; www.legacyhotels.co.za [7 C3] These are new super-luxurious apartments opened in 2005 in an unbeatable location overlooking Nelson Mandela Square. The 1–3 bedroom suites, spread over 4 floors, are better aimed at corporate people on long stays, with hi-tec kitchenettes in stainless steel and dark wood, enormous flat-screen TVs, and entertainment systems with surround sound, wireless internet, and very stylish contemporary décor with South African modern art on the walls. Facilities include pool, gym, sauna and steam rooms, and a delightful roof garden with views across Sandton. The whole block is fingerprint accessible throughout. *Rates start from R3,200, and if you don't want to make your own, again b/fast is taken at the Michelangelo hotel across the square.*

Rivonia B&B (9 rooms, 12 units) 3 River Rd, Rivonia, Sandton; ☎ 011 803 2790; www.rivoniabb.co.za [1 D3] Charming guesthouse in a very large garden. The units have private entrances and are equipped with kitchenettes, modern décor, minibars, Mnet TV, fans and under floor heating. Breakfasts are served on the patio overlooking the swimming pool. This is a good value option for Sandton; set in a quiet cul-de-sac with lots of trees and birds. *Rates from R550.*

🏠 **Sandton Sun and Towers Inter-Continental** (525 rooms, 35 suites) corner Fifth St and Alice La, Sandhurst; ☎ 011 780 5000; www.southernsun.com; www.johannesburghotels.intercontinental.com [7 C2]
This is an enormous hotel with wireless internet in every room. Décor is modern and stylish and extras include phones in the bathrooms and fresh fruit. There are several restaurants, 2 swimming pools, a health club and one of the largest conference facilities in the country (that can accommodate 10,000 people). Everything is arranged in 2 towers linked by a skywalk and with direct access into Sandton City shopping mall, and there are great views of Johannesburg from the upper floors. Has all the facilities and services you can expect of a 5-star hotel; they even provide bodyguards for VIPs. *Room rates start from R1,780.*

🏠 **The Saxon Hotel** (20 luxury Egoli suites, 2 presidential suites and 2 platinum suites) 36 Saxon Rd, Sandhurst; ☎ 011 292 6000; www.thesaxon.com [7 A2]
Hidden in the residential suburbs, this wins hands down at the luxury end for its individuality, character and setting. Surrounded by lovely rolling lawns and giant trees, the first thing you'll notice is the enormous rim-flow pool when you are driven up to the door from the car park by limo. Rooms are individually furnished and the décor reflects the art and crafts of Africa, and there are some wonderful pieces on display. Rooms have big-screen DSTV, DVD and CD players with surround-sound systems, and minibars. A frequent award winner, it has formerly won world's best boutique hotel in a number of competitions. The hotel was home to Nelson Mandela for a few months after he was released from prison and it's where he wrote *The Long Walk to Freedom*. *Room rates start at R4,250, rising to over R15,000 for the platinum suites.*

⌂ **Tladi Lodge** (10 rooms, 2 suites) 1 David St, Sandton; ☎ 011 784 9240; www.tladilodge.co.za [7 D1] Tladi's rooms are arranged in lovely low thatched buildings surrounding a sparkling pool, which are more personal than the larger hotels, with a country-style atmosphere in large grounds. Rooms are luxurious with all the mod cons, and are individually decorated. Guest lounge with fireplace, library, no restaurant but close enough to Sandton's nightlife. A peaceful option. *Rates vary but start at R980.*

City Lodge Morningside corner Hill and Rivonia Rds, Morningside; ☎ 011 884 9500 [7 C1]
City Lodge Sandton corner Katherine St and Grayston Dr, Sandown, Sandton; ☎ 011 444 5300 [7 E2]
Courtyard Suite Sandton 130 Rivonia Rd, Sandown, Sandton; ☎ 011 884 5500 [7 D2]
The Don Sandton I 3 Rivonia Rd, Sandton; ☎ 011 268 6606 [7 B4]
The Don Sandton III 125 Pretoria Av, Sandton; ☎ 011 883 5814 [7 D2]
The Don Sandton IV 115 Pretoria Av, Sandton; ☎ 011 883 5814 [7 D2]
Garden Court Morningside corner Rivonia Rd and Cullinan Cl, Morningside; ☎ 011 884 1804 [7 C1]
Garden Court Sandton corner Katherine St and Rivonia Rd, Sandhurst; ☎ 011 884 5660 [7 C3]
Garden Court Sandton City corner West and Maude Sts, Sandown; ☎ 011 269 7000 [7 C2]
Road Lodge Rivonia corner 10th Ave and Rivonia Rd, Rivonia; ☎ 011 803 5220 [1 D3]
Town Lodge Sandton corner Grayston Dr and Webber Rd, Sandown, Sandton; ☎ 011 784 8850 [7 D2]

ROSEBANK AND AROUND

⌂ **10 Bompas** (10 suites) 10 Bompas Rd, Dunkeld West; ☎ 011 325 2442; www.tenbompas.co.za [7 A1] A fine boutique hotel tucked down leafy Bompas Rd within walking distance of Hyde Park Mall. Very stylish modern décor throughout with fine pieces of African art on the wall or displayed on pedestals, with stunning interior design, and an award-winning restaurant serving gourmet food which is widely regarded to be one of the best in the country (listed under *Eating and Drinking*), with a wine cellar that contains over 4,000 bottles. The garden is peaceful and full of large trees and there's a swimming pool. They also own a couple of luxurious camps in Kruger, so the well-heeled can combine a stay here with a safari. *Rates are R2,400 for sgl and dbl.*

🏠 **The Grace** (73 rooms) 54 Both Av, Rosebank; ✆ 011 280 7200; www.grace.co.za [8 B3]
Very elegant upmarket hotel in the heart of Rosebank Mall with a wonderful balconied stairwell. Rooms are spacious and luxurious with marble bathrooms and fat towelling dressing gowns; the mattresses have zips so can be twin or dbl. Facilities include beauty spa and gym, guest lounges, a restaurant and a fabulous roof garden with a lawn, benches, sun loungers and a rather unique swimming pool that runs the length of the building. *Included in the rates, which start from R2,700, are treats like coffee and cake or neck massages, and free mobile phone rental.*

🏠 **Melrose Arch Hotel** (118 rooms) 1 Melrose Arch Sq; ✆ 011 214 6600; www.africanpridehotels.com [8 D1]
Located at trendy Melrose Arch with its shops, popular restaurants and offices, this is a new 5-star hotel with designer rooms, and is one of Jo'burg's hippest places to stay. Everything is very hi-tec and the rooms have flat-screen TVs, DVD players and internet points, as well as 21 lights in each that you can play around with to change the mood. The restaurant is superb (listed separately under *Eating and drinking*) and there are a number of bars, including one in the library with big fat leather armchairs, and one actually in the swimming pool. An unusual feature is the avenue of trees planted in giant tin buckets. Very stylish throughout. *Rooms start from R1,950.*

🏠 **Park Hyatt** (244 rooms) 191 Oxford Rd, Rosebank; 📞 011 280 1234; www.johannesburg.park.hyatt.com [8 B2] Quality luxury hotel with an enormous black-tiled lobby and shiny black glass windows. Facilities include a health club with saunas and steam rooms, swimming pool, a 24-hr business centre, and the Zafferano lounge and restaurant (dealt with under *Eating and Drinking*). The hotel is connected to the Firs Mall, which you can walk through to get to the Rosebank Mall. *Rates start from R1,785.*

🏠 **The Peech Hotel** (6 rooms) 61 North St, Melrose North; 📞 011 537 9797; www.thepeech.co.za [8 C2] Another stylish addition to Melrose, this attractively designed boutique hotel has wonderfully decorated rooms with polished wooden floors, bright red and orange furnishings, flat-screen satellite TVs, spacious designer bathrooms, white cotton sheets, feather duvets and subtle lighting. French and Spanish is spoken, there's wireless internet, a pretty garden with swimming pool, a bar and a deli-style restaurant that serves up some delicious and delicately presented food. Very chic and professional, and good value at *R1,100 per room.*

🏠 **Rosebank Hotel** (300+ rooms) corner of Tyrwhitt and Bath Av; 📞 011 447 5817; www.rosebankhotel.co.za [8 A3] This is an older hotel with a good reputation, popular with tour groups and within walking distance of the shopping malls. All rooms are equipped with DSTV and pay movie channels and internet access; the suites have additional bars and lounges and two restaurants, one of which is the very good Chinese Lien Wah. *Rates start from R1,060.*

🏠 **Protea Hotel Wanderers** (200 rooms) corner Corlett Dr and Rudd Rd, Illovo; 📞 011 770 5500; www.proteahotels.co.za [8 C2]

5

This very modern and hi-tec hotel is at a busy road junction but is very conveniently located within a stone's throw of Wanderers' Cricket Stadium. Rooms are comfortable with all mod cons; a special touch is that a fresh apple is delivered to your room daily. Facilities include a swimming pool, a very trendy 24-hr cocktail and deli bar, a good restaurant, wireless internet on the ground floor, and there's a gym around the corner. *Rates start from R1,000 though good deals can be done through the website when there's no cricket on.*

🏠 **The Westcliff** (106 rooms, 14 suites) 67 Jan Smuts Av, Westcliff, to the south of Rosebank; ☎ 011 646 2400; www.westcliff.co.za [3 E1]

The Westcliff is located near the Johannesburg Zoo and has wonderful views from the terrace across northern Jo'burg, and it is from this vantage point that you realise how green the city is. The bright pink hotel is a landmark on Jan Smuts Av. All rooms and suites are equipped with AC, VCR players, internet and fax lines, all arranged in cottages spreading down the hillside. Facilities include 2 heated swimming pools, floodlit tennis court with resident coach, gym with personal trainers and a health spa. The 2 restaurants are very good and the cosy wooden panel bar with large armchairs is the perfect spot for a nightcap, even if you're not staying. *Rates vary from R2,100 to well over R8,000.*

🏠 **Courtyard Suite Rosebank** corner Oxford Rd and Tyrwhitt Av, Rosebank; ☎ 011 880 2989 [8 B2]
🏠 **The Don Rosebank** 10 Tyrwhitt Av, Rosebank; ☎ 011 8801666 [8 A3]

🏠 **Backpackers Ritz** 1A North Rd, Dunkeld West; ☎ 011 325 7125; www.backpackers-ritz.com [8 A1]

Jo'burg's oldest and most popular backpackers' with accommodation for up to 70 people in dbls or dorms and more peaceful B&B accommodation around the corner. Within walking distance of Hyde Park Mall, kitchen for self-catering or basic meals available, bar, swimming pool, large rambling house with *koppies* for good views, very helpful travel centre for travel all the way up to Nairobi, and they run their own excellent tour company for half- and full-day tours to all the sights. *Dorm beds are R85 and dbls R260.*

MELVILLE AND PARKHURST

⌂ **33 on First** (7 rooms) 33 First Av, Melville; ☎ 011 726 7172; www.33onfirst.co.za [3 B2]
Friendly B&B with simple décor, prints on the walls and wicker furniture, satellite TV, small swimming pool and thatched outside entertainment area surrounded by palms; generous b/fasts. *Rooms from R500.*

⌂ **A Room with a View** (12 rooms) 1 Tolip St, corner 4th Av, Melville; ☎ 011 482 5435;
www.aroomwithaview.co.za
This is a rather striking castle-like building high on a hill with fantastic views of the northern suburbs. Some rooms have their own conservatory, balcony and fireplace. It's very nicely decorated with wrought iron furniture and picture windows, and there's a marvellous indoor swimming pool surrounded by pillars. B/fasts will keep you going all day and Melville's restaurants and shops are within walking distance. *Rooms from R660.*

⌂ **Bridge House** (5 rooms) 7 Third St, Parkhurst; ☎ 011 880 1111; www.africaadventure.co.za
A very unusual house that has the Braamfontein River (although it's more like a wide stream) running alongside it, and there's a wrought-iron bridge equipped with ornate lanterns crossing from the house to the gardens. 5 spacious en-suite rooms overlooking the river and garden, the décor is almost entirely white except

for the Persian carpets; internet access, Mnet TV and kettles in the rooms. Walking distance to the restaurants in Greenside. *Rates from R750.*

🏠 **The Space** (4 en-suite rooms) 62 Fifth Ave, Melville; ☎ 011 726 7885; thespace@mweb.co.za [3 A1]
A very pleasant guesthouse set in a low chocolate-brown building within walking distance of the bars and restaurants. Modern comfortable décor; each of the rooms has a private entrance, CD players and minibar, and two have small kitchenettes. *Rates from an affordable R500.*

🏠 **Garden Court Milpark** corner Empire and Owl Sts, Auckland Park; ☎ 011 726 5100 [3 B3]

BRAAMFONTEIN AND CITY CENTRE

🏠 **Parktonian** (300 rooms) 120 De Korte St, Braamfontein, just off Rissik Street; ☎ 011 403 5740; www.parktonian.co.za, www.proteahotels.co.za [4 F4]
The unmistakable Parktonian tower has operated in the city centre since the mid 1980s. At the time of writing it had been completely overhauled and the individual suites were sold off to investors who use them themselves or put them back into a hotel room 'pool' to be let to regular guests. Good standard hotel furnishings and facilities with restaurant, bar, indoor swimming pool and undercover parking. *Rates start from R460.*

🏠 **Sunnyside Park Hotel** (110 rooms) Princess of Wales Ter, Parktown; ☎ 011 643 7226; www.legacyhotels.co.za [4 H2]
This is one of the closest hotels to the city centre but it is in a secure suburb and set in lovely mature

gardens with enormous trees. The original building is an 1865 Victorian manor which is now a national monument, and the communal areas have a lot of atmospheric wood panelling, old prints and gilt mirrors on the walls and fireplaces. The rooms, though spacious, have recently been refurbished, so have lost the charm of the older architecture but are nevertheless comfortable with all the usual facilities. Milner's restaurant is for formal meals and the Penny Pub with its long bar and wooden deck is for drinks and light meals. There's a swimming pool, small gym, large secure car park, and wireless internet. *Rates are R880.*

SOWETO

These days there are a number of homes in Soweto that rent out rooms on a B&B basis and there are currently 56 rooms available for tourists. Whilst all the rooms are very similar, they are hosted by friendly people keen to promote Soweto as a tourist destination, and many are close to the sights such as the Mandela Museum and the Hector Pieterson Memorial and Museum. Some are listed below, or alternatively visit the website of the Soweto B&B Association (*www.sowetobedandbreakfast.co.za*) to browse through the photos and book accommodation. Most are reasonably priced; expect to pay around R250–500 for a double including a cooked breakfast. If you are driving enquire about safe parking or ask about transfers. Alternatively discuss with your tour operator about being dropped off after your Soweto tour.

Botle Guest House and B&B (3 en-suite rooms) 648 Monyane St, Dube; ☎ 011 982 1872 [2 B3]
A tidy brick house with neat lawns. Rooms are furnished with satin bed covers and fitted wardrobes, nicely

decorated dining room and lounge, TV room, secure yard for parking, close to Wandie's, Soweto's most popular restaurant.

🏠 **Ekhaya Guesthouse** (3 rooms, 2 en-suite) 8027 Bacela St, Orlando West; ☎ 011 939 2850 [2 A3]
Furnishings are modern and bright and the house overlooks Desmond Tutu's house. There is safe parking and dinner is served on request.

🏠 **Lebo's Backpackers** (4 dbl rooms, 2 dorms) Powe Street, Soweto, between Mzimhlophe and Phomolong train stations; ☎ 011 326 1700; www.sowetobackpackers.com
You can camp in the garden, there is a self-catering kitchen (though meals are also provided) and a comfortable lounge with TV and stereo. Tours of Soweto can be arranged, and Lebo, a very friendly young man, will show you around, arrange drumming sessions and even take you to local football matches.

🏠 **Neo's B&B** (1 sgl room, 1 dbl room) 8041 Bacela St, Orlando West; ☎ 011 536 0413; www.soweto.co.za [2 A3]
Again near Desmond Tutu's house and the Mandela Museum, this neat red-bricked house has smart furnishings and there's a comfortable lounge plus a lovely *lapa* (thatched entertainment area) in the garden.

🏠 **Thuto's B&B** (4 rooms) 8123 Ngakane St, Orlando West; ☎ 011 936 8123 [2 A3]
Just next door to the Mandela Museum with parking behind walls under a car port, large lounge with TV, the furnishings are very elaborate with enormous headboards, ornate dressing tables, chaise longue and 3 bathrooms.

🏠 **Vhavhenda Hills B&B** (1 dbl room, 1 twin room) 11749 Mampuru St, Orlando West; ☎ 011 936 0411 [2 A3] Again centrally located in Orlando West within walking distance of the sights. Rooms are colourfully furnished in a bright white house behind a huge pine tree. Traditional African b/fasts including *snoek* (fish) are on offer.

🏠 **Wandie's Place** (7 rooms) 618 Makhalemele St, Dube, Soweto; ☎ 011 982 2796; www.wandiesplace.co.za Modern en-suite rooms in a tidy brick house on the street behind the restaurant (see page 94) with AC, DSTV, phone, smart furnishings, secure parking and fully stocked bar.

6 Eating and Drinking

The restaurant scene in Johannesburg is the best in Africa and there is a vast choice of all cuisines and atmospheres. Eating out is easily one of the highlights to the city and still represents good value for money for the visitor when you consider the fabulous food, wonderful décor and unbeatable service. Jo'burgers themselves love to eat out regularly and have high expectations of what they want from a good restaurant. In the northern suburbs, lunch is a huge deal, not only with business people, but with the thousands of housewives that meet daily with their friends to gossip and examine each other's false nails. At the weekends brunch is popular, when the usually besuited execs swap into casual clothes and read the newspapers, preferably at a table in the sun.

Service is important in South Africa and every table gets its own 'waitron' who looks after the diners throughout the meal. Unlike places in Europe these days, there is no self-service and you pay for everything at the end, even if it's just a cup of coffee. The waiting staff are of a very high calibre and should be quite rightly tipped about 10%. It's a proper professional job in South Africa and waiters often join waiting lists to work in the best restaurants. And Jo'burgers themselves are particularly susceptible to 'restaurant rage' if they receive anything but top class service.

There are thousands of restaurants in Johannesburg and the list below is only a selection of recommended eateries that are established and popular with locals and tourists alike. Some are world famous such as Gramadoelas or Carnivore and make a fine addition to any tourist's itinerary, others have award-winning cuisine and wine lists, whilst others are simply Jo'burg residents' reliable old favourites. This really is just the tip of the iceberg. For more information about restaurants once in Johannesburg, pick up a copy of the latest *Eat Out* magazine available at the airport and all branches of Exclusive Books, which reviews all the good restaurants in the city.

The places I have listed are all independent restaurants with character, good food and something a little special about them. Johannesburg is of course also full of the ambiguous chains where menus are standardised and the décor in each one is the same. Although I am not going to bother to provide addresses, they are widespread; fast-food joints like KFC and Wimpy, Nandos (grilled chicken), Nino's (coffee shop and panini type sandwiches), Spur Steakhouses (family steak restaurants), Panarotti's (pizza and pasta), Ocean Basket (seafood and fish), and Steers (fast food, burgers and steaks). There are also countless coffee shops throughout the northern suburbs and in the shopping malls; again, far too many to list, but be assured there's plenty of choice, and as well as a full range of coffees and teas, they also serve light meals, salads and sandwiches.

Many of the restaurants are in the shopping malls, but thanks to good designs and positioning, you will be unaware that you are sitting in a shopping mall. This is especially true of Nelson Mandela Square in the Sandton City mall, which is a lovely atmospheric place to eat out. Some restaurants are in the big hotels that are also open to non-guests, and others are huddled together in certain neighbourhoods with tables spilling out onto the pavements. Melville is the oldest restaurant haven and over several blocks, along 7th Street from 1st to 5th avenues, there are numerous restaurants and little bars, and this is the best place to head for if you're looking for nightlife. Other popular spots are the roundabout on Gleneagles Road in Greenside, where there are several of Johannesburg's best restaurants, 4th Avenue in Parkhurst, and 7th Avenue in Parktown North. Just go to any of these places and wander up and down the streets until you find something that takes your fancy. On the other side of the city in Cyrildene is Chinatown, a now well-established street of very authentic Asian restaurants. There are many restaurants in Soweto, and the likes of the original Wandie's, a Soweto institution, are likely to be visited as part of a tour. Finally all of the casinos have several restaurants as well as food courts (see page 112).

CITY CENTRE AND SOWETO

✗ **Gramadoelas** Bree St, Newtown; ☎ 011 838 6960; www.gramadoelas.co.za [5 E6]
This restaurant has a special place in Johannesburg's culinary history that has hosted thousands of tourists over the years, including Queen Elizabeth II, Nelson Mandela, and a spattering of celebrities such as Elton John and David Bowie. Apparently when Denzel Washington visited, staff kept calling him Malcolm X! Samples from the menu include *snoek*, a popular fish in South Africa; *bobotie*, a local version of shepherd's pie with Cape

Malay spices and a savoury custard topping; *umngqusho*, braised beef shin, beans and maize; game meat such as kudu with dried fruit and spices or deep fried crocodile tail; and (not for the faint-hearted) *mopani* worms. These are popular in southern Africa as a nutritious and free source of protein (though oddly the Zulu people won't touch them) and are served in a tomato relish with spinach. Desserts include ice cream served with prickly pear sauce and traditional South African *milktert*. There are also dishes from north Africa on the menu and the use of herbs and spices is inventive and delicious. The cosy lightly lit décor is a mix of African art and antiques, plus some theatre memorabilia such as a photograph of Miriam Makeba, one of South Africa's most famous songstresses, in an orange dress which she wore in the 1950s that was designed by the restaurant's owner. Everything is arranged under high ceilings with chandeliers and there's also a grand piano and brass lamps that once were owned by the Oppenheimer family. The service is impeccable and the waiters can talk you through the menu. If there's something good on at the nearby Market Theatre, combine a visit here with a show for a fine night out. The word *Gramadoelas* means 'back of beyond' in the San language. *Average main course R70; open Tue–Sat 12.00–15.00, 18.00–23.00, Sun 18.00–23.00.*

✕ Guildhall Pub ☎ 011 836 5560 [6 F6]

The original one-storey building was built in 1888 soon after gold was discovered and served the early miners. The long wooden bar has been stripped and polished and it has been decorated in period furnishings with wooden tables and red leather stools, and photographs of the city's early years adorn the wood panelled walls. *Open daily Mon–Fri 11.00–late, Sat 11.00–19.00.*

✕ Kapitan's ☎ 011 834 8048 [5 E7]

This is an Indian restaurant that was a favourite of Nelson Mandela when he was a young lawyer in the

1950s. It was opened over (a rather staggering) 90 years ago and is still going strong today and the curries are legendary. Amongst the football stickers, bull-fighting posters and Chinese lanterns that decorate the walls, look out for the letter from Mandela to the restaurant whilst he was in prison saying how much he missed the food. Other famous patrons include Jackie Onassis, the Shah of Iran, and Eva Perón of Argentina. *Open daily for lunch 12.00–14.00, although on Sat it's advisable to be there before 13.30.*

✗ **Wandi's Place** 618 Makhalamele St, Dube, Soweto; ☎ 011 982 2796; www.wandies.co.za
This was the first restaurant in Soweto to become popular with tourists and is a mandatory stop on most Soweto tours. It started out as an illegal *shebeen* in 1991 and even today owner Wandile Ndala still cooks the buffet spread. Famous visitors include Richard Branson, Brad Pitt and the New Zealand All Blacks rugby team. During lunchtime there's a good vibe as everyone on the tours sits at long tables and chats. The restaurant is self-service and traditional township dishes are on offer such as tripe and oxtail, chicken and mutton stews, *pap* (mealie porridge), rice and dumplings, and rather delightfully desserts are a throw back to school dinner days with trifle, jelly and custard on the menu. Look out for the 'networking wall' where many thousands of visitors have pinned their business cards or currency from their own country. *Average main course R70; open 07.00–21.00.*

MELROSE ARCH

✗ **March** 1 Melrose Arch Sq; ☎ 011 214 6666; www.africanpridehotels.co.za [8 D1]
Restaurant in the *uber* stylish Melrose Arch Hotel, headed by a female celebrity chef who has previously overseen the cooking of 20,000 meals at the MTV music awards in Europe. Décor is cutting edge, with

SOUTH AFRICAN DISHES

ACHAAR Imported to South Africa by migrant Indians; a spicy salad made of mango and oil.

BILTONG Dried and salted raw meat similar to beef jerky in the US.

BOBOTIE Curried mince with an egg sauce on top which is baked.

BOEREWORS A traditional spicy and coarse sausage made of beef or lamb.

CHAKALAKA A salad of Indian origin made of onion, garlic, ginger, green pepper, carrots and cauliflower and spiced with curry and chilli.

FRIKKADEL The South African version of a meat ball.

KOEKSISTERS Traditional Afrikaner, plaited, sticky and syrupy dough cakes.

PAP Boiled corn meal, a common staple all over Africa.

ROOIBOS TEA A herbal caffeine-free tea made in the Cape.

SNOEK A tasty local fish that is usually smoked. A snoek braai, or barbecue, is a popular pastime.

indoor and outdoor seating, and a comfortable bar. The menu is pretentious fusion, and one wonders if you can really mix the likes of 'grilled salmon fillet on welted greens, sweet potato mash, green pea *wasabi* and shanghai vinegar jus', but nevertheless the food is delicious and delicately presented. Apart from the prawns, all dishes are the same price – R95 for 1 course, R175 for 2, R225 for 3 – so prices effectively come down the more you eat. The desserts are to die for and there are some wicked chocolate ones, including the chocolate brownie with double white chocolate ice cream. *Average main course R95; open 12.00–15.00, 18.30–23.00.*

✗ The Meat Co. 6 Melrose Sq, Melrose Arch; ☎ 011 684 1787; www.themeatcompany.co.za; there's another branch at Montecasino [8 D1]

Comfortable modern décor with large dining areas and outside terrace. A central feature of this restaurant is the tower of 3,000 wine bottles centred around a spiral staircase. Serves a good range of meaty fare such as steaks, lamb shanks, pork spare ribs, spatchcock chicken and fish, though there's only one option for vegetarians, which is the platter of vegetable kebabs and deep fried cheeses. Good range of *pedros* (ice cream and a tot of alcohol), liqueur coffees and brandies. There are other branches in Australia and Dubai. *Average main course R65; open 12.00–22.00.*

✗ Moyo Melrose Sq, Melrose Arch; ☎ 011 684 1477; www.moyo.co.za [8 D1]

This is an award-winning restaurant and one of the best eating experiences in Johannesburg. It serves Pan-African food from all over the African continent, cooked by a team of top-class chefs, and this is really an eating extravaganza spread over 5 themed floors. There are several set menus to choose from, which are ideal to share and include east African coconut curries, spicy Tunisian *mezes*, Nigerian soups, and South African seafood. There's cutting edge designer décor throughout; comfortable brown leather sofas in the cigar lounge, a fully authentic Moroccan tent, wonderful mosaics and brass art, and ochre-stained walls and wooden ceiling in the wine cellar. Most of the decoration is African themed and even the staff wear wonderfully traditional African cloth and have painted faces. Ladies come around the tables to give diners henna tattoos, 'wishy washy' women bring bowls and wash your hands whilst singing, and Zimbabwean musicians strum a personal melody at your table on a guitar. This is a combination of art, design, performance and fine food. It's a magical experience. There's another smaller branch at the Market Theatre in Newtown (☎ 011 838 1715), and another in Zoo Lake (☎ 011 646 0058), with a lovely outside terrace, but the Melrose Arch branch has the best *wow* factor. *Average main course R175; open 12.30–14.30, 18.30–22.00.*

ROSEBANK AND PARKTOWN NORTH

✘ **Baccarat** Mutual Sq, Tyrwhitt Av, Rosebank Mall; ☎ 011 880 1835 [8 B3]
French bistro serving à la carte dishes and good value, all-you-can-eat buffets with specials such as grilled ostrich, crocodile stew and oxtail in red wine. Classy antique-like décor, subdued lighting and cosy corners make it a good spot for a romantic dinner, though the food is very rich. *Average main course R85; open 12.30–15.30, 18.00–22.30, closed for lunch at the w/ends.*

✘ **Bombay Blues** Rosebank Mall; ☎ 011 447 3210 [8 B3]
Upmarket Indian restaurant specialising in *tandoori,* with melt-in-your-mouth curries and breads; try the paper-thin rotis to mop up the richly flavoured sauces. Best to share a few dishes amongst a group and don't over-order as the portions are huge. The classic butter chicken is delicious. *Average main course R65; open 12.00–14.30, 18.30–22.30.*

✘ **Café Tribeca** Rosebank Mall, near the cinema; ☎ 011 447 3281 [8 B3]
In the middle of the mall but conveniently located close to the cinema, so it's a good spot for coffee or a glass of wine before or after a movie. Serves a huge variety of trendy coffees, fat muffins and brownies, and light meals such as burgers, pastas and salads. *Open 08.00–23.00.*

✘ **Cranks** Rosebank Mall, Rosebank; ✆ 011 880 3442 [8 B3]
Another firm favourite in the northern suburbs located near to the African Craft Market, with an unpretentious and relaxed atmosphere and affordable menu. The décor is very bright and colourful and the metal tables spill out onto the street. Look out for the naked Ken and Barbie dolls hanging from the ceiling in compromising positions! The food is Thai and Vietnamese; firm favourites are green and red curries plus a full range of seafood and vegetarian dishes. Drinks include shots of schnapps (try the grapefruit one) and a range of imported Asian beers. *Average main course R50; open 11.00–16.00, 18.00–23.00, closed Mon.*

✘ **The Grillhouse** The Firs Mall, Oxford Rd, Rosebank; ✆ 011 880 3945 [8 B3]
Another excellent steak restaurant where there's a wide choice of basted or pepper-coated steaks accompanied by good vegetable selections and piping hot sauces. There's also some seafood, but it's limited for vegetarians. The décor is chunky bare brick with heavy wooden furniture and the atmosphere is vibey as it's popular with large groups, and you can end the evening with a cigar and whiskey at the impossibly trendy Katzy's across the way (see page 117). *Average main course R80; open 12.00–14.30, 18.30–23.00, no lunch on Sat.*

✘ **La Belle Terrasse and Loggia** the Westcliff Hotel, 67 Jan Smuts Av; ✆ 011 646 2400 [3 E1]
Perched at the top of the cliffs at the wonderful Westcliff Hotel, this terrace certainly has one of the city's most beautiful views overlooking the green northern suburbs and the zoo. The décor, in quiet pastels, is elegant and unabashedly colonial. The Sunday brunch is legendary, with a buffet that includes French oysters, caviar, queen prawns, smoked salmon and eggs Benedict. In the evening musicians move amongst the tables playing accordions and violins. *Average main course R180; open 07.00–10.00, 12.30–14.30, 19.00–22.30, brunch on Sun, 11.30–14.00.*

✘ Wombles 17 3rd Ave, Parktown North; ✆ 011 880 2470

I used to live in Harare, Zimbabwe, and fondly remember Wombles as a place to get the best steak in town. The restaurant has been forced to move south because of problems in Zimbabwe and has made a successful home in a finely converted house in Johannesburg. Carnivores should head here for kilo portions of protein, rich sauces, specials such as roasted quail, and fine wines all served in rooms decked out in atmospheric, dark polished wood with leather high-back chairs. *Average main course R90; open Mon–Sat 12.30–14.30, 18.30–21.30, no lunch on Sat.*

HYDE PARK

✘ Fournos Bakery Dunkeld West Centre, corner Jan Smuts Av and Bompas Rd, Dunkeld; ✆ 011 325 211; www.fournos.co.za [8 A1]

This is the most famous bakery in the northern suburbs, popular with suited businessmen and backpackers from the Backpackers' Ritz just up the road during the week, and is the place to be seen for b/fast over the w/end. The bakers work throughout the night to produce a vast variety of fresh bread and rolls, quiches, cakes, pastries, sausage rolls and samosas, and the spit-roasted chicken is legendary. The b/fasts are excellent, *macon* is substituted for bacon for vegetarians, light meals and good coffee are on offer and there's an extensive deli counter. Despite the outside tables overlooking a packed row of cars in the car park, it is consistently full and you may have to wait for a table. There's also a branch in Fourways Crossing mall and at the airport. *Average main course R35 and lots of cheap eats; open Mon–Fri 07.00–18.00, Sat 06.00–16.00, Sun 06.00–14.00.*

✵ **Osteria tre Nonni** 9 Grafton Ave, Craighall Park; ☎ 011 327 0095

A sophisticated Italian restaurant with a huge range of homemade pasta and creamy sauces, though the rather boring décor could do with a revamp. The house speciality is the *gamberoni gorgonzola*, grilled giant tiger prawns with gorgonzola sauce, and they serve *porcini* mushrooms drizzled in garlic, and *foie gras* pan fried in orange juice and cognac. *Average main course R90; open Tue–Sat 12.30–14.00, 19.00–22.00.*

✵ **The Red Chamber** Hyde Park Corner mall, Jan Smuts Av, Hyde Park; ☎ 011 325 6048 [8 A1]

On the upper floor of the mall, this is a high-quality Chinese restaurant with attentive service and traditional red lantern type of décor. Good for groups to share a range of starters and mains as there are 'lazy susans' in the middle of the tables. Old favourites include sliced beef in chilli sauce, ginger prawns, calamari in black bean sauce and good old Peking duck with all the trimmings, and lots of options for vegetarians. The Beijing style of cooking is very spicy, so be careful when choosing. *Average main course R70; open 12.00–22.00.*

✵ **Sides** Ten Bompas Hotel, Bompas Rd, Dunkeld; ☎ 011 325 2442; www.tenbompas.com [8 A1]

This very elegant restaurant in a boutique hotel has a fine reputation and soothing décor, with many African objets d'art on display. For fine dining it's not overly expensive and the unfussy flavoursome dishes concentrate on the freshest seasonal ingredients. The wine cellar boasts an impressive collection of over 4,500 bottles. The bathrooms are communal. *Average main course R70; open 07.00–10.00, 11.00–14.30, 18.30–22.30.*

✵ **Willoughby's** Hyde Park Corner mall, Jan Smuts Av, Hyde Park; ☎ 011 325 5107 [8 A1]

On the ground floor of the mall, this place is literally stuffed full of fish and seafood all on display in the chilled glass cabinets. You can pick out want you want and have it cooked in a variety of ways or choose from the à la carte menu. There are changing specials of daily line fish, and the prawns and calamari are reliably good. Tables look out over the not very scenic environs of the mall, but nevertheless the food is good and not unreasonably priced for seafood. *Average main course R75; open Mon 11.30–15.00, Tue–Sun 11.30–22.00.*

ILLOVO

✕ **Thrupps** Thrupps Shopping Centre, corner Oxford and Rudd Rds, Ilovo; ☎ 011 268 0298; www.thrupps.co.za [8 C1]
The grocers of distinction, Thrupps first opened a shop on the corner of Eloff and President streets in 1892. Despite relocating since then, it's still the oldest shop in Johannesburg. The First National Bank presented the shop with a clock on the 100th anniversary of it being a customer of the bank. Today it's in Ilovo and is Jo'burg's answer to London's Fortnum and Mason, which sells an extensive range of deli food, seafood, champagnes and fine wine, poultry such as pheasant or quail, smoked salmon, caviar and imported cheeses. The staff are wonderful (many of them have been working here for decades) and the picnic baskets are legendary. They also sell gifts and homeware. *Open Mon–Fri 07.45–18.00, Sat 08.00–14.00, Sun 09.00–13.00.*

✕ **Yamato** 196 Oxford Rd, Ilovo; ☎ 011 268 051 [8 B1]
An elegant restaurant with white-linen-clad tables serving a long menu of perfectly presented sushi with a good wine list and imported Japanese beer. During lunchtime there are set menus and on Sunday they offer family specials to inaugurate the little ones in the art of eating sushi. *Average main course R100; open 12.00–14.30, 18.30–22.30, closed Sat lunch.*

SANDTON

✘ **Bread Basket** Village Walk mall, Rivonia Rd, Sandton; ☎ 011 883 9886; and at Sandton City ☎ 011 783 9053 [7 D2]

A superb deli with counters stuffed full of pâtés, cold meats, breads and rolls, cakes and pastries, and some wicked desserts. The sandwiches are freshly made, as are the still-warm giant muffins. *Open 08.00–19.00.*

✘ **Browns of Rivonia** 21 Wessels Rd, Rivonia; ☎ 011 803 7533; www.browns.co.za [1 D2]

Established restaurant with a consistently good reputation set in an old farmhouse with a patio overlooking a peaceful garden. Large groups can opt to eat in the wine cellar, and there's a cheese room where you can go and choose what cheese to put on your platter. The menu is extensive, with everything from roast lamb to a seafood platter, and although on the expensive side at around R500 for a meal for two with wine, you'll be assured of a good feed. *Average main course R90; open Mon–Fri 12.30–22.30, Sat 18.30–22.30, Sun 12.30–15.30.*

✘ **Bukhara** first floor, Nelson Mandela Sq, Sandton City; ☎ 011 883 5555; www.bukhara.com [7 C2]

The original Bukhara is in Cape Town and now this excellent north Indian restaurant has a home in Nelson Mandela Square. Without doubt serving the best Indian food in the country, the company also produces a range of frozen curries and sauces sold in the supermarkets. It's not cheap but the food is superb, with a full range of aromatic and flavoursome curries and *tandoori* dishes, and they have incorporated South African game meat such as kudu into the menu. The kitchen is behind glass so you can watch the chefs at work, and each dish is made from scratch. There is an extensive, albeit expensive, wine list and the service in the dark wood interior is first class. *Average main course R150; open 12.00–15.00, 18.00–23.00.*

✘ **The Butcher Shop and Grill** Nelson Mandela Sq, Sandton; ☎ 011 784 8776; www.butchershop.co.za [7 C2]
South Africa is well known for its good steak, and in my opinion this is the best steak restaurant in the country. It's a lovely spot with outside tables overlooking the gorgeously lit square, and the inside bar is a great spot for a pre-dinner drink. This is where to head for a melt-in-the-mouth fillet and a bottle of hearty red wine, or you can get a steak tartar with a shot of cognac. There is a good range of sauces and side dishes, such as roasted beetroot or baked pumpkin, and steaks are cut to the size of your liking. Pork, lamb and plentiful seafood such as oysters and Scottish salmon also feature on the menu, and there are some good salads, though there's not much specifically for vegetarians. Beef cuts can be bought from the butchery and they'll vacuum pack them for you. *Average main course R90; open 12.00–22.30.*

✘ **Exquisite Tastes** Grayston Shopping Centre, Sandton; ☎ 011 784 6737; www.exquisitetastes.co.za [7 D2]
Another excellent deli with very stylish stainless steel décor, packed from wall to ceiling with jars and tins of delectable items such as lemon curd or melon jam, and lemongrass or asparagus. Breakfasts, light meals and snacks are available. The owner also runs regular dinner evenings which involve the guests getting involved with the cooking. *Open Mon–Fri 08.30–17.30, Sat–Sun 09.00–13.00.*

✘ **O'Galito** Village Walk mall, Maud St, Sandton; ☎ 011 783 4930 [7 C2]
This is another award winner that has played host to famous food presenter Ainsley Harriott, who filmed a show for BBC Food here. It's a modern formal restaurant, with Brazilian jazz playing in the background, and

CHINATOWN

Derrick Av, Cyrildene

Jo'burg's Chinatown is located on both sides of Derrick Avenue in Cyrildene and although it's a fairly seedy area, eating out here is an inexpensive and fun night out. There's no need to make a reservation – simply walk up and down until you find a restaurant that takes your fancy. Hardly any of the owners speak English and many of the menus are in Chinese, so you will have to enlist one of the waiting staff to help you order. Most restaurants are a little shabby; tables are formica-topped, there are dead ducklings hanging in the windows, and the glasses and cutlery don't always match. But the food, which arrives on big steaming plates, is superb, very authentic and ridiculously cheap: tender pork ribs in sweet sauce, chicken with cashew nuts, crab with ginger and spring onion, big bowls of clear soup with pork and shrimp-filled dumplings and Chinese greens, larger-than-average *maki* sushi rolls, and plenty of Peking duck all washed down with Korean beer. The bill is often written down on a napkin at the end of a meal, and if you've finished and they need the table, you will be shooed out. Kitchens close early, at around 21.00, credit cards are not accepted and you need to take your own wine. There are car guards to watch your car.

it's best known for its seafood, especially the excellent prawn and crab curries with a *peri-peri* Mozambique influence. There's a pleasant bar area and some tables look down into the mall. *Average main course R70, seafood platters considerably more; open 12.00–14.30, 18.00–22.30.*

✗ **Vilamoura** Sandton Sun Intercontinental Hotel, corner of Fifth St and Alice La, Sandhurst, Sandton; ☎ 011 884 0360 [7 C2]

Considered one of the city's best Portuguese/seafood restaurants and is famous for its expensive but excellent seafood platters. It is smart and quite formal, with a cream and gold interior and art prints decorating the walls. In addition to seafood, the *piri piri* chicken and Portuguese steaks and casseroles are also good. *Average main course R150; open Mon–Fri 12.30–23.00, Sat 18.30–23.00.*

✗ **Wangthai** Nelson Mandela Square, Sandton; ☎ 011 784 8484 [7 C2]

On the first floor overlooking the lovely square, a high quality Thai restaurant with exquisite, delicately presented food and intimate service. The menu is endless, with green and red curries, fish cakes, noodle dishes and salads. Food is prepared by a team of Thai chefs. *Average main course R50; open 12.00–14.30, 18.00–22.00.*

✗ **Yo Sushi** Village Walk mall, Maude St, Sandton; ☎ 011 7836166 [7 C2]

Small but very trendy sushi bar with modern light wood and metallic interior where the conveyer belt bar is stacked with boxes by the hard-working chefs. *Sashimi, nigiri* and *maki* sushi are on offer at the counter or you can order hot *teppanyaki* from the kitchen, and there's plenty of *saké* and green tea to accompany your meal. *Average main course R80; open 11.00–22.00.*

GREENSIDE

✗ **Bela Fonte** 10 Gleneagles Rd, Greenside; ☎ 011 646 3502

Portuguese restaurant on the trendy Greenside strip, serving excellent fish or beef *espetadas* on vertical skewers, good steaks with fried eggs planted on top, lots of seafood, and *chorizo* sausage doused in brandy. The food's very meaty and rich, so expect to feel completely full. *Average main course R65; open 12.00–late, closed Sun eve.*

✕ **Circle Restaurant and Champagne Bar** 141 Greenway, Greenside; ☎ 011 646 3744
Located on the popular Greenside restaurant strip and behind twinkling lights in the trees outside, this is a very trendy eatery with a buzzy atmosphere which is light and airy with modern art on the walls. There's a good selection of cocktails, over 25 vodka-based martinis, and, as the name suggests, fine French champagne, and the food is nouveau cuisine with an Asian influence; salmon on a bed of *wasabi* mashed potatoes for example. *Average main course R80; open 12.00–15.00, 19.00–22.30.*

✕ **Icon** 51 Greenfield Rd, Greenside; ☎ 011 646 4162
Another Greenside gem. Although not wholly Greek, most dishes are Mediterranean influenced and there's an excellent variety of *mezes* and lamb dishes, with a few Thai dishes thrown in for confusion. The décor is fairly staid but the staff are easy going and the food is quite delicious. Try the seafood soup for a treat, with langoustine and queen prawns, or the lamb shank served with mint sauce. Chocolate boxes are offered for dessert. *Average main course R80; open Tue–Sun 12.00–15.00, 18.45–22.00, no dinner on Sun.*

✕ **Karma** corner Barry Hertzog and Gleneagles Rds, Greenside ☎ 011 646 8555; corner 7th and 3rd Avs, Parktown North: ☎ 011 447 1094; shop 11, 24 Central, corner Gwen Lane and Fredman Dr, Sandton [7 C2]
Good Indian restaurant with three branches, all with modern décor, Indian art on the walls and giant Buddhas overlooking the tables. Food includes traditional *tandooris* and *biryanis* as well as a Western twist on favourites

such as *samosas* which are filled with cream cheese and salmon or feta and spinach, and excellent vegetarian dishes such as butternut pumpkin, peanut and coconut curry. *Average main course R65; open Tue–Sun 12.30–15.00, 18.00–22.00.*

✕ **Yum** 26 Gleneagles Rd, Greenside; ☎ 011 486 1645
This is consistently voted as one the Johannesburg's top restaurants for the quality of the food and the chef has been awarded more trophies than the national football team and has published his own cookery book. The décor is nothing to write home about, with bare walls and simple white table-clothed tables, but the food is delicious and inventive and served with style and flair; think big plates small portions. But what it lacks in size it makes up for in taste. Here's an example to whet the taste buds; a sashimi of fresh Scottish salmon, filled with goose liver and pistachio nut pâté, presented with a salad of cress leaves and roasted apples dressed with cognac syrup. *The average price for a two-course meal with wine is about R500 for two and an average main course R90; open Mon–Sat 12.30–14.30, 18.30–21.30, no lunch on Mon.*

MELVILLE

✕ **Pomegranate** 79 3rd Av, Melville; ☎ 011 482 2366 [3 A1]
Another Melville success story, this restaurant is arranged in several small rooms in a charming cottage creating a cosy and intimate atmosphere. The menu changes regularly but there's always a good choice of red meat, venison, fish and poultry and they are famous for their tomato tart starter. After dinner head to any one of the nearby bars. *Average main course R80; open Mon–Sat 12.00–14.30, 19.00–23.00, no lunch on Sat.*

COFFEE CONNECTIONS

There are several chain coffee shops around Johannesburg that now also have wireless internet access. Check out the websites for locations.

Mugg & Bean 011 339 2675; www.muggandbean.co.za. Excellent coffee shops with the same menu in each and famous for bottomless cups of freshly roasted coffee, though coffee is served in a variety of ways – hot, cold, iced, whipped, blended or decaffeinated. Light meals are available in 5 day sections: early morning, b/fast, lunch, dinner and late-night. *Open 07.30–22.30.*

News Café 011 883 4629; www.newscafe.co.za. A full range of alcoholic and non-alcoholic drinks, including the very tempting peanut butter double mocha cappuccino and a full range of daiquiris. The menu features wraps, nachos and meat and vegetarian dippers. The cafés tend to become more bar-like as the evening progresses. *Generally open 08.00–24.00.*

Seattle Coffee Shop 011 325 4642 for nearest branch; mostly attached to branches of Exclusive Books with the same opening hrs. A great concept of bookshop cafés, featuring steel chairs and tables and large brown leather sofas where you can flick through a magazine or weigh up the new titles. There's a full range of coffees, giant cookies and muffins, and other decadent treats.

✕ **Soi** corner 7th St and 3rd Av, Melville; 011 726 5775 [3 A2]
This is Melville's best Asian restaurant with a relaxed and laid-back atmosphere. There's a wide range of Thai and Vietnamese food and it's very affordable. The curries are good, as is the excellent starter *meamg khum;*

dry-roasted coconut, chilli and lemongrass rolled in small spinach cones. You might want to pass on the *angry duck* though, as it's viciously hot. *Average main course R70; open 12.00–14.15, 18.00–22.00.*

BEYOND THE CITY

✖ **Carnivore** 69 Drift Bld, Muldersdrift, off the N1; ☏ 011 957 3132
Over the top, touristy and very popular given that it can seat 500 people, but nevertheless a fun, gut-busting excursion. About 15 different types of meat are roasted on *Masai* spears over a central fire pit. A very hot cast iron plate is placed in front of you, followed by two *potjiekos* (pots) containing *pap* (boiled corn porridge) and sauce, and the waiters come around slicing meat on to your plate until you surrender. Soup and dessert are also included. Some of the tour operators offer transport out here. *Set lunch R135, dinner R155; open 12.00–16.00, 18.00–24.00.*

✖ **The Harvard Café** Terminal Building, Rand Airport, Germiston, access from the N3; ☏ 011 827 0251; www.harvardcafe.co.za [2 E3]
This is an enormous restaurant with tables on terraces overlooking the runway of Rand Airport to the east of the city. For anyone with an interest in aviation it's well worth the drive out and it's hugely popular with families at the w/end and on Friday and Saturday when there's live music. From your table you can see all the airport's traffic and the brooding South African Airways 747 that has been parked here since its decommission from the Jo'burg–Perth–Sydney run in 2003. The Sunday buffet breakfast accompanied by violin and cello players is legendary, as are the excellent pizzas from the wood-fired oven and a very long menu of just about every meal imaginable. Service can be slow because of the crowds, but it's a good place to relax

over a few beers and prices are very reasonable given the huge portions of food. Planes that regularly take to the air are L29 fighter jets, Tiger Moths, Harvards, Pitts and various helicopters. From the office you can arrange short flights in a number of aircraft, from R200 for a few minutes. *Average main course R50; open daily 08.30–late.*

FCO TRAVEL ADVICE
know before you go
fco.gov.uk/travel

Bradt Travel Guides is a partner to the 'know before you go' campaign, masterminded by the UK Foreign and Commonwealth Office to promote the importance of finding out about a destination before you travel. By combining the up-to-date advice of the FCO with the in-depth knowledge of Bradt authors, you'll ensure that your trip will be as trouble-free as possible.

www.fco.gov.uk/travel

7 Entertainment and Nightlife

For information about what's on, check the newspapers or visit the arts section of the *Mail & Guardian* newspaper's website, www.mg.co.za, or visit www.tonight.co.za. All tickets for theatres, cinemas and sports events (and even bus tickets) can be booked directly or online through Computicket (*www.computicket.co.za*). This is a national booking service and there are Computicket kiosks in the shopping malls.

CINEMA

All the cinemas are in the shopping malls and casinos, with several screens and food courts for popcorn and cool drinks (as the South Africans call soft drinks). As the malls open in the morning there are several screenings throughout the day until late at night. Tickets cost about R35, and one day a week tickets are half price (usually Tuesdays). If you have pre-booked online through Computicket, increasingly the cinemas have swipe machines for your credit card to pick up tickets. These are the main cinema chains; info on what's on and when can be found on the websites:

Ster-Kinekor www.sterkinekor.com. Regular Hollywood and home-grown movies.

Nu Metro www.numetro.co.za. Same as above.

Cinema Nouveau also found at www.sterkinekor.com. Has a cinema at Rosebank Mall and shows off-beat and gritty art-house cinema and foreign films, and regularly hosts film festivals.

CASINOS

During the years of apartheid gaming was illegal in South Africa but legal in the former black homelands. During the 1970s and 1980s many casino resorts were built in the homelands attracting white gamblers from the cities on long day or overnight trips. Some of these locations were quite incongruous. Sun City is a perfect example – it was built in the middle of nowhere and is a three-hour drive from Johannesburg. Since the breakdown of apartheid gaming has become legal throughout the country and new casino resorts are springing up outside all of the major cities. These don't just offer gambling, but are full-on entertainment centres for the whole family, and have other attractions such as food courts, theatres, shops, nightclubs, hotels, cinemas and other things to do unrelated to gambling. The casino at Gold Reef City is, for example, next to the Gold Reef City theme park and the Apartheid Museum (see page 196 and page 172) and Montecasino is also the location of an excellent bird park (see page 200).

Between them the casinos below have over 8,000 slot machines and almost 300 gaming tables. They are hugely popular and are packed to the gills at the weekend. Believe it or not I used to be a croupier in London (in another life) where membership rules in casinos are much more restricted than in South Africa. In my mind, gambling in South Africa is unwisely promoted under the guise of family entertainment, with entry allowed for everyone; the result is that there is certainly an issue of problem gambling. Despite the fact that the casinos promote responsible gambling (*'winners know when to stop'*), and do not allow anyone under 18 onto the actual gaming floors, they also offer lessons on how to play and provide facilities such as crèches, cinemas or video game arcades to keep children occupied. The problem is that these children will think nothing of patronising the gaming areas as soon as they turn 18, simply because more often that not they have grown up spending considerable time in these complexes with their parents anyway.

Nevertheless there is certainly something for everyone to do and all the casinos are big, brash, modern and glitzy, and are open 24 hours. It is worth visiting one just to see the over-the-top décor; Montecasino has been built in the style of a full-on Tuscany town, whilst the Emperors Palace features more Roman columns than the Colosseum.

☆ **Carnival City** corner Century and Elsburg Rds, Brakpan, off the N17 heading east of Johannesburg; ☎ 011 898 7000; www.suninternational.com/Resorts/CarnivalCity. Casino, six-screen cinema, kids' adventure playground, 2 hotels, 5 restaurants, a food court and 3 bars.

☆ **Emperors Palace** 64 Jones St, Jet Park, Kempton Park, near the airport; ☎ 011 928 1000; www.emperorspalace.com. Casino, 2 hotels (see pages 75–6), theatre, show bar, nightclub, nine restaurants, cocktail bar, food court and a health spa.

☆ **Gold Reef City** 14 Shaft, Northern Parkway Dr, Ormonde; ☎ 011 248 5000; www.goldreefcity.co.za [2 C3] Casino, Gold Reef City theme park (see page 196), 2 hotels, 5 restaurants, food court and theatre.

☆ **Montecasino** corner William Nicol Dr and Witkoppen Rd; ☎ 011 510 7000; www.montecasino.co.za [1 C2] Casino, 15-screen cinema, theatre, 6 bars, bird gardens (see page 200), kids' play centre, skate park, 15 restaurants and a food court.

THEATRE

Johannesburg has a wealth of venues, and there are varied performances from indigenous drama, music and dance to imported West End and Broadway hits, classical opera, and ballet. The newly rejuvenated Newtown area, with the Market Theatre and jazz venues, is well worth a visit now the area has been made safe for visitors. The casino theatres often play host to cabaret, and the Civic Theatre features visiting musicals from overseas.

Barnyard Theatre Broadacres Shopping Centre, corner Cedar Av and Valley Rd, Fourways; ☎ 011 467 9333; www.barnyardtheatre.co.za [1 C2]

The Boma Theatre corner Ring and Fore Rds, Alberton; ☎ 011 869 2666; www.theboma.co.za [2 E4]

Civic Theatre Loveday St, Braamfontein; ☎ 011 877 6800; www.showbusiness.co.za [4 F4] Includes the Nelson Mandela Theatre, the People's Theatre and the Tesson Theatre.

The Colosseum Showbar and Theatre of Marcellus Emperors Palace, 64 Jones St, Jet Park, Kempton Park; ☎ 011 928 1000; www.emperorspalace.com

Globe Theatre at Gold Reef City Gold Reef City, corner Northern Parkway; ☎ 011 248 5168; www.goldreefcity.co.za [2 C3]

Johannesburg Youth Theatre 3 Junction Av, Parktown; ☎ 011 478 1778; www.at.artslink.co.za [4 F3]

Liberty Theatre on the Square Nelson Mandela Sq, Sandton; ☎ 011 883 8606; www.at.artslink.co.za [7 C2]

Market Theatre corner Bree and Wolhuter Sts, Newtown; ☎ 011 832 1641; www.markettheatre.co.za [5 E6] Includes the Laager Theatre, the Barney Simon Theatre and the Main Theatre.

Off Broadway Supper Theatre 59 Grant Av, Norwood; ☎ 011 403 1563; www.peoplestheatre.co.za

Pieter Toerien's Theatre Montecasino, corner William Nicol Dr and Witkoppen Rd, Fourways; ☎ 011 511 1818; www.montecasinotheatre.co.za [1 C2]

The Showcase Banbury Cross Shopping Centre, Hans Strydom Dr, Northwold, Randburg; ☎ 011 794 4382; www.theshowcase.co.za

Wits University Theatre Complex corner of Jorissen and Station sts, Braamfontein; ☎ 011 717 1372; www.wits.ac.za/paa [3 D4] Includes Wits Downstairs Theatre, Wits Amphitheatre, and the Nunnery.

NIGHTLIFE

Jo'burgers love to party and the big night out in South Africa is Saturday, closely followed by Thursday and Friday. Many of the restaurants already listed become more alcoholic as the evening wears on and most are just as popular venues for drinking as they are for the food, so the division between bar and restaurant is often blurred. The most stylish restaurant bars are at Moyo, the Polo Lounge at the Westcliff Hotel, and the bar at the Park Hyatt.

JOHNNY CLEGG

One of South Africa's best-loved musicians is Johnny Clegg, who was born in the UK in 1953 and emigrated with his family to South Africa at the age of nine. When he was 13 or 14 he began to learn to play the guitar and after a chance meeting with a street guitarist near Clegg's Johannesburg home, he swapped from classic Spanish guitar music to Zulu music. He began to go secretly into the townships and visit the men's migrant workers hostels to practise his guitar and learn to dance, which on one occasion led to his arrest for contravening the Group Areas Act. His reputation reached the ears of Sipho Mchunu, a migrant Zulu worker who had come up to Johannesburg in 1969 looking for work. He wanted to meet this young white boy who could dance like an African and play Zulu street music. Their friendship sparked when Johnny was 16 and Sipho was 18, and between them they wrote songs that fused Zulu rhythms and Western lyrics, most with a strong protest element. They went on to form the group Juluka, meaning 'sweat' in Zulu, but as a mixed-race group they were constantly badgered by the authorities, and attempts were frequently made to ban or censor their music in South Africa. Despite this they released several albums, and with their anti-apartheid lyrics sung in both English and Zulu they had great success touring the rest of the world. Juluka now regularly tour South Africa, and Johnny and the boys (*www.johnnyclegg.com*) put on a great show with music and storytelling about their experiences. By the end they get the whole audience up on their feet.

If you can't decide where to go head for the streets around 7th Avenue in Melville in the northern suburbs. Here there are plenty of bars and clubs close enough together which are ideal for a pub crawl. You can also go through one of the tour operators and arrange a night-time tour of Soweto, which includes dinner and visits to some of the lively *shebeens* (pubs). Listed below are some of the most popular nightspots, but in a city the size of Johannesburg nightlife comes and goes depending on trends. Up-to-date listings can be found at www.jbhlive.co.za. Expect to pay in the region of R20–70 to get into the clubs.

LATE BARS

♀ **Catz Pyjamas** corner 3rd and Main Rds, Melville; ☏ 011 726 8596 [3 B2] Cocktail bar and restaurant that's an ideal place for a late snack and is Jo'burg's original 24-hr after-party spot; located in a lovely old building with an iron balcony where you can watch the sun come up over b/fast. The décor is funky, and the nachos and sangria are legendary. *Open 24hrs.*

♀ **Cool Runnings** 27 4th Ave, Melville; ☏ 011 482 4786 [3 B2] This reggae-themed bar and restaurant is hugely popular with the younger set. Outside is a bar under thatch and wooden tables, and there are plenty of rooms to prowl through whilst nursing a beer. Loads of shooters and cocktails are also available and there is occasional live comedy. *Open daily 12.00–late.*

♀ **Katzy's at the Grillhouse** The Firs, Oxford Rd, Rosebank; ☏ 011 447 5162 [8 B3] Located in the Firs mall, Katzy's has based itself on two piano bars in the US — Jillys in Chicago, once owned by Frank Sinatra, and Don't Tell

Mama's Piano Bar on the Upper West Side in New York. There are lots of chunky bricks, fat armchairs and art deco sofas, soft blues music, and a top-of-the-range selection of cigars, whiskies and cognacs. A DJ livens things up after 22.00. The crowd leans towards the middle aged, but they are impossibly trendy. *Open Mon–Sat 17.00–late.*

♀ **Tanz Café** Riverside Centre, Bryanston Drive, Riverside; ☎ 011 463 3128 [1 D3] This is a combination of a European and Argentinean dance café where you can practise your tango to passionate music on the large dance floor. They also play appropriate music for salsas, mambos, cha cha chas and rhumbas. A seasonal menu is on offer, you can accompany your dancing with tea and cake in the afternoon and cocktails in the evening, and there's a comfortable bar and tables around the dance floor to relax at if you prefer to watch others doing the dancing. Look out for the live music and cabaret evenings. *Open Mon–Sat 09.00–late.*

♀ **The Radium Beer Hall** 282 Louis Botha Av, Orange Grove; ☎ 011 728 3866; www.theradium.co.za [2 D1] This is the oldest pub in Jo'burg and has been going strong since 1929. The bar is the original bar from the Ferreirastown Hotel, from the early mining-camp days, and is over 100 years old, and the walls are covered in memorabilia. It's got a great atmosphere, is stoked with history, there's live music 4 nights a week, and the 19-piece Radium jazz band plays on the first Sunday of each month. The Portuguese inspired menu is great too, with delicious *prego* rolls, excellent ribs, 1kg of prawns for R150 and a wide selection of local and imported beers. *Open Mon–Sat 10.00–midnight.*

♀ **Tokyo Star** 78a 4th Av, Melville; ☎ 011 442 9812 [3 A1] A vibrant, eclectic, funky bar with a wide variety of music supplied by DJs from 21.00, Mon–Sat. Japanese pop culture décor with lots of neon, a good range of spirits and beers, large sofas in the windows and sushi available to snack on. *Open 12.00–late.*

♀ **Xai Xai** 7th St, Melville; ☎ 011 482 6990 [3 A1] This popular street in Melville boasts several bars, but Xai Xai is one of the best. It's an artsy, late-night watering hole popular with media types, with a Mozambican theme (Xai Xai is a beach resort north of Maputo). Excellent African music, some of the best grilled prawns in Johannesburg, and a long cocktail menu with drinks named after famous people, including Graça Machel (the widow of the former Mozambican president), who is now married to Nelson Mandela. *Open 11.00–02.00.*

CLUBS AND LIVE MUSIC

♀ **Back o' the Moon** Gold Reef City Casino, Northern Parkway Dr, Ormonde; ☎ 011 496 1423; www.goldreefcity.co.za [2 C3] Back o' the Moon was a famous Sophiatown *shebeen* in the 1950s which experienced an explosion of jazz that attracted black and white people to listen to the great South African stars such as Miriam Makeba. Today the name has been taken by a large venue with funky décor at the Gold Reef City Casino with a very good restaurant, 2 bars, a private dining room and a dance floor, and there's live jazz on most nights. More suited to an older crowd looking for a dinner/dance experience, but it has also been host to South African *Idols* (the TV talent show) events which attract teenagers. *Open Tue–Sun 12.00–14.30, 18.00–22.30.*

♀ **Bassline** 10 Henry Nxumalo St, Newtown; ☎ 011 838 9145; www.basslinejazzclub.co.za [5 E6] For nearly a decade Bassline had its home in Melville before moving into the Newtown Music Hall in 2005. The new Bassline has now got a club and concert hall with a 1,000-person capacity, which regularly hosts South Africa's top jazz, kwaito and hip-hop artists. Very mixed crowd, all colours and ages, and a lively spot to get down to some great music. Tickets vary in price depending on the artist; check what's on when through Computicket.

♀ **Carfax** 39 Pim St, Newtown; ☏ 011 834 9187; www.carfax.co.za [5 D6] This arts centre is open during the day for its changing exhibitions and fine art gallery, and is also used for poetry readings and literary group meetings. Then at the weekends it opens as a club until the early hours with a wide range of music from garage to Brazilian, mostly geared towards the younger and gay crowd. There are three spacious dance floors, top DJs playing a diverse mix of music, and regular party nights. Note this is in one of Newtown's dodgiest and grimiest streets, so exercise caution after dark, though the venue attracts hundreds of people on popular nights. *Open Mon–Fri 09.00–18.00, Fri–Sat 21.30–late.*

♀ **Horror Café** 15 Becker St, Newtown; ☏ 011 838 6735 [5 E6] This is a vibrant nightspot playing reggae on Thursday, and jazz and African music such as kwaito at the w/ends. The décor is rather striking horror-movie memorabilia. Aspiring DJs from Johannesburg's DJ Academy try out here and there are occasional dance performances. *Open Thu–Sat 21.00–late.*

♀ **Monsoon Lagoon** Emperors Palace Casino, 64 Jones St, Kempton Park; ☏ 011 928 1280; www.monsoonlagoon.co.za. Very stylish, fashionable nightclub with extravagant décor and lighting, and lots of treats such as bubble-making machines, projection screens, VIP lounges, and lots of hi-tec equipment to recreate the effects of avalanches, lightning or volcanoes. There's also a team of sexy professional dancers, male and female, that strut their stuff on catwalks and podiums. Probably the flashiest and glitziest club on the continent, the Monsoon is a sophisticated and fun night out, though you'd better be dressed to kill. *Open Wed–Sat 21.00–late.*

♀ **Roxy's Rhythm Bar** 20 Main Rd, Melville; ☏ 011 726 6019 [3 B2] One of Melville's most established clubs and very popular with students at weekends. Music varies depending on the night and there are sometimes live bands. Indeed many of the more successful local bands began life at Roxy's. It has recently been refurbished with better acoustics and a bigger stage. *Open Mon–Sat 20.00–late.*

♀ **Songwriter's Club** corner Quinn and Carr Sts, Newtown; ☏ 011 833 1317 [5 D6] This club, in a building once used by the old Premier Milling Company, is now a laid-back place where budding songwriters can air their talents in public. They're mostly hip-hop artists from the townships. The venue has a restaurant, bar, VIP lounge and a stage with a well-equipped sound system. The reception area, with its sheets of metal and wood, has been designed to feel like a shack, creating an atmosphere reminiscent of the backstreet venues where new music is born. *Open Tue–Sat 18.00–late, entertainment starts at 21.00.*

♀ **Taboo** 24 Central, Gwen Ln, Rivonia, Sandton; ☏ 011 783 2200; www.taboo.co.za [7 C2] Stylish club with opulent décor, popular with Sandton's elite and a frequent host for local celeb gatherings and launches. You'll need to dress up to get in, there are several bars and 2 dance floors, and music tends to be commercial, which means you may actually recognise some of the tunes. *Open Thu–Sat 21.00–late.*

♀ **The Blues Room** Village Walk, corner Rivonia and Maud Sts, Sandton; ☏ 011 784 5527; www.bluesroom.co.za [7 C2] The Blues Room has earned itself a rightful reputation as a top-class live music venue, and has regularly been voted the best jazz and blues venue in Johannesburg. Local and international bands perform most nights a week, the food's very good and you can dance in front of the stage. *Open Tue–Sat 16.30 in the bars, 19.00 in the restaurant till late.*

♀ **The Rock** 1987 Vundla St, Rockville, Soweto, just off the Old Potchefstroom Rd; ☏ 011 986 8182. This is a popular Soweto club for kwaito and jazz, with a large bar area and dance floor, and a roof deck with fabulous views of Soweto at night. There is ample parking with security, and the restaurant serves wholesome traditional township cuisine such as chicken stew and *pap*. The house speciality drink is a 'Soweto kiss', a mix of whisky, bourbon and lime – administer with caution. The décor is very trendy, with chrome counters which are chilled to keep your drink cool, and images of Jo'burg are projected on the walls. *Open Mon–Fri 21.00–23.00, Sat–Sun 21.00–02.00.*

GAY JOHANNESBURG

South Africa is generally very gay-friendly and has a forward-thinking constitution that legalised same-sex adoptions in 2003 and gay marriages in 2005. In fact in 2005 Johannesburg made a bid for the 2010 Gay Games, but lost out to Cologne in Germany. However, the age of consent for gays and lesbians in South Africa is 19 as opposed to the heterosexual age of 16. Although Cape Town is the pink capital of Africa, Johannesburg has a thriving gay scene and the annual Gay Pride celebrations are now into their 17th year. These usually happen in September around Newtown where there is a parade, and music and cabaret events, held at various venues. The South African Out in Africa gay film festival is held in March. Johannesburg produces a Pink Map available at the tourist offices, though this has not been updated recently. The best sources of information are the websites below. Gays are generally openly affectionate in most of the restaurants and bars, though of course specifically gay nightclubs come and go regularly, as in any large city. Again, check out the websites for up-to-date info.

www.mask.org.za covers gay affairs throughout Africa.

www.gaynetsa.co.za lists clubs, bars and gay-friendly accommodation (and celebrity gossip).

www.q.co.za is South Africa's main gay and lesbian website with entertainment news, a dating service and chat rooms.

www.oia.co.za Out in Africa gay film festival.

www.mambaonline.com features, news, clubs and what's on, celebrity gossip and dating.

SPORT

Johannesburg has a wealth of venues to both watch and play sport; South Africans are sports mad. Traditionally in South Africa, rugby and cricket, in which South Africa is successful internationally, used to be the enclave of the whites, whilst soccer was predominantly black supported and the national team, *Bafana bafana*, frequently does well in African tournaments. But this is changing rapidly and sport is increasingly multi-cultural these days. South Africa has previously been host to both the rugby and cricket world cups, and is presently gearing up for its role as host nation for the 2010 FIFA World Cup. Johannesburg is home to the two leading venues for the latter; Ellis Park and Soccer City (or FNB Stadium after its sponsors, First National Bank). Soccer City is hosting both the opening match and the final. It is set to be enlarged from its present seating capacity of 80,000 to 94,700. Ellis Park is hosting one of the semi-finals with a capacity of 70,000. All sporting events, like theatre tickets, can be booked through Computicket (*www.computicket.com*), though for the football world cup, another system for booking tickets is expected to be put in place.

CRICKET

The Wanderers Cricket Stadium Corlett Dr, Illovo; ☎ 011 788 1008; www.cricket.co.za [8 C1] Good old Wanderers is one of the world's best cricket pitches, which hosted the 2003 Cricket World Cup final between India and Australia.

LIPIZZANER

Dahlia Rd, Kyalami, off the N1 north of Johannesburg; ☎ 011 702 2103; www.lipizzaner.co.za [1 D1]; 60min show every Sun, 10.30; R70 adults, R40 children, R60 senior citizens, tickets can be booked through Computicket (www.computicket.co.za) or bought at the door.

Most people have heard of the world-renowned Spanish Riding School in Vienna with its beautiful white stallions performing to music every Sunday morning. But not many people know that they also perform every Sunday morning in Kyalami, one of Jo'burg's otherwise indistinctive northern suburbs. This is the only other school of performing Lipizzaner stallions in the world to be given the seal of approval by Vienna's Spanish Riding School. After fleeing his native Hungary after World War II, Count Jankovich-Besan, his family, and his beloved Lipizzaner stallions settled on a farm in Natal. A Polish cavalry officer, Major George Ivanowski, also emigrated to South Africa, and met the

It has a capacity of 33,000, there's plenty of parking and there are regular fixtures throughout the summer.

GOLF There are over 40 golf courses in and around Johannesburg. The ones listed below have been recommended to me by Johannesburg golfers as the best. Visitors should expect to pay around R180–350 green fees and golfers will need a handicap and to be dressed smartly.

Count, who offered him Lipizzaners to train. The first stallion was called Maestoso Erdem, which became the first Lipizzaner in South Africa to perform *Haute Ecolé* (translated directly to 'high school' in French, but also means the art of difficult horsemanship). From there he began developing an equestrian centre at Kyalami, and in 1969 he built the first indoor hall for training the horses. Today there are regular Sunday performances at the Lipizzaner Centre in a vast hall which measures 60m x 20m, with tiered seating at one end. Interestingly, whilst the mares are not considered to have enough of a presence for performances compared to the stallions, the team of riders are all female. This is a classical dressage show, in time to classical music, in which the horses skip, trot on the spot, side step, high step, and jump off the ground and kick with their back legs at the same time – an act that was meant to decapitate enemies in war situations. The horses are elegant, graceful and dignified, and they love performing.

Bryanston Country Club Bryanston Dr, Bryanston; ☏ 011 706 1361 [1 C3] Founded in 1948 in the heart of Sandton's residential area this is an impeccably kept course with lots of fine trees and good birdlife. It's a challenging par 73 course with a lot of water hazards.

Glendower Golf Club Marais Rd, Edenvale; ☏ 011 453 1013. This course is located in the upmarket suburb of Bedfordview. It's an obstacled par 72 course with 85 bunkers and water features at 11 of the 18 holes.

Pecanwood Golf and Country Club 40-min drive from Johannesburg towards Magaliesberg, next to the Hartbeespoort Dam; ☏ 011 706 8066: www.hartbeespoortdam.com/pecanwood. One of the best and prettiest courses in the region, surrounded by the picturesque Magaliesberg Mountains and designed by Jack Nicklaus. By all accounts Nicklaus has a penchant for bunkers, of which there are hundreds covering a total 5ha of the par 72 course. The 13th hole juts into a lake.

Royal Johannesburg Golf Club Fairway Av, Linksfield North; ☏ 011 640 3021–4 [2 E1] Over 100 years old, this club was granted the royal bit by King George V in 1931, and in 1933 a second 18-hole course was added. Over the years it has frequently hosted the South African Open, which has previously been won by South African native Gary Player, one of the greatest golfers of all time.

Vodacom World of Golf corner Woodmead and Maxwell Sts, Woodmead; ☏ 011 802 5864; www.worldofgolf.co.za [1 E2] This is not a course as such but a professional practice facility with a driving range with greens and bunkers, 4 practice greens, a 9-hole chip and putt course and a teaching academy, all surrounded by pretty gardens and waterfalls.

Wanderers Golf Club corner Corlett Dr and Rudd Rd, Illovo, next to the Wanderers Cricket Stadium; ☎ 011 447 3311 [8 C1] Centrally located in the northern suburbs, this is a scenic par 72 course and in the past it has been host to the South African PGA Championship.

GYM There are gyms all over Johannesburg and most offer temporary membership to visitors. Some also have beauty salons and child-minding facilities. For locations and more information visit:

Planet Fitness www.planetfitness.co.za. *Open 24hrs.*
Virgin Active Gyms www.virginactive.co.za

RUGBY AND SOCCER

Ellis Park Stadium corner Currey and Staib Sts, Doornfontein; ☎ 011 402 8644 [6 K5] This stadium hosts rugby and soccer and the occasional rock concert. Ellis Park's greatest moment came when it hosted the Rugby World Cup final in 1995, which was won by South Africa's Springboks. The cup was presented to the team by a jubilant Nelson Mandela wearing a green Springbok jersey. Ellis Park's worst moment came in 2001, when, tragically, 43 people were killed in a crush during a football match. Although there is some parking and plenty of car guards in the surrounding streets, space is limited and it's not a great area of the city security-wise. It's best to make use of the park-and-ride service offered by the stadium, where you leave your car at various car parks elsewhere and get a bus to and from the stadium. This can also be booked through Computicket (*www.computicket.com*).

Johannesburg Stadium 124 Van Beek St, Doornfontein; ℡ 011 402 8644 [4 K4] Originally built as an athletics stadium, this stadium is now the home ground of one of South Africa's best-loved soccer teams, the Orlando Pirates. Its excellent acoustics also make it popular for other open-air events and concerts. The All Africa Games were held here in 1999.

Soccer City Nasrec Rd, Nasrec; ℡ 011 494 3640; www.fnbstadium.co.za [2 B3] Also known as the FNB Stadium after its bank sponsors, this is the country's largest sports stadium, which is in the process of being made bigger in preparation for the 2010 Football World Cup. It was built in 1987 on the outskirts of Soweto and just about the whole of Soweto is euphoric that the World Cup opening ceremony and the final will be played on their doorstep. It's the home ground of the Kaizer Chiefs (not to be confused with up-and-coming rock band the Kaiser Chiefs) and the South Africa Football Association. There's a great atmosphere here, especially during a Johannesburg derby between the Chiefs and the Pirates — and don't worry about parking, there's plenty.

SWIMMING Most of Johannesburg's hotels have swimming pools. There's also a very nice open-air public pool in **Zoo Lake Park** (℡ 011 646 8754; open 07.30–18.00 during summer; see page 202) and an Olympic-sized heated pool at the **Ellis Park Stadium** (℡ 011 402 5565; open Mon–Fri 06.30–21.00, and Sat 06.30–18.00; see above).

8 Shopping

Johannesburg has shopping for Africa. Indeed many Africans from neighbouring countries regularly visit just for the shopping and an estimated 300,000–400,000 migrant shoppers visit the city each year. For the international visitor, the choice of shopping is vast, not for just crafts and curios but for international brands and designer labels. Compared to Europe, prices are comparable or a little lower for most things such as food, electronics, clothing, diamonds, gold, jewellery, leather goods and African curios and art. The exception to this is books, which tend to be more expensive than Europe as they are mostly imported. Tourists have the added benefit of claiming back the 14% VAT on items when they leave the country (see page 52), which is worth considering when pricing things.

Most of the shops are located in the giant super malls, of which there are over 20 around Johannesburg (a selection is listed below). These not only have shops, but cinemas, restaurants, post offices, supermarkets, pharmacies and banks – in fact they have anything from internet cafés and nail technicians to hairdressers and tattoo artists. The phrase 'shoppertainment' is used to describe these, and most warrant at least a half-day's outing if you are serious about shopping. Shops in the malls are generally open daily from 09.00 to 18.00 whilst the restaurants and cinemas are open until 23.00. In the listings below I have indicated opening hours; these are for the shops not the restaurants. All have car parks where you will pay a small hourly fee or pay a car guard. At the time of writing a R1 billion project had been announced to turn the old power station in Orlando, Soweto, into a mega mall. This is a huge upturn in investment for Soweto; it will provide 10,000 jobs and it's likely to be one of the city's biggest malls. There are also many smaller shopping centres dotted around the city listed on the maps, which will have a few shops, cafés and perhaps a supermarket serving the local neighbourhood.

Listed below are some of the South African chain shops found in most malls. Other international chains that feature in the top-of-the-range malls include Levi's, Body Shop, Diesel, Guess, Tommy Hilfiger, Gucci, Hugo Boss, Louis Vuitton, and Polo, amongst many others (but we still don't have Gap!). For those serious about fashion head to Sandton City, Rosebank mall and Hyde Park Corner, where along with the international brands you'll find a fine showcase of South African designers. In all of these there are some marvellous places to have lunch or to stop for a café latte.

For specialist items such as crafts and curios, Johannesburg has a good variety of flea markets and these make for a good day out, especially over summer as they also have stalls selling snacks and often there is children's entertainment on. There is an excellent range of good quality African souvenirs on offer such as wooden sculptures and masks, cloth, items crafted from wire and beads, drums, stools etc and if you are buying from the markets, unlike souvenir shops, there is the opportunity for a bout of good-humoured haggling. Johannesburg's best market for crafts is the African Craft Market at the Rosebank mall where good quality items from all over the continent are for sale, and there are a number of good galleries. As well as the markets, also look out for things for sale along the side of the road, especially in the northern suburbs. Many local entrepreneurs set up shop along the side of the road selling anything from slabs of turf to bean bags and dog kennels, and occasionally there are souvenir sellers.

CHAIN STORES

DEPARTMENT STORES

Clicks www.clicks.co.za. This is South Africa's answer to the UK's Boots, selling toiletries, homeware, electronics, sunglasses and cosmetics. It has only recently added pharmacies.

Woolworths www.woolworths.co.za. This is not the old red Woolworths found in the UK and the US selling toys, sweets and stationery but it is in fact a chain that is almost identical to Marks & Spencer in the UK, selling quality clothes, homeware, food and wine. It's hugely popular in South Africa. The story goes that M&S did not want the world to know that they were trading in South Africa during apartheid when there was an international boycott going on, so they traded under the name Woolworths which didn't already exist there. Their food is superb but not cheap, and some of the larger stores offer deli counters where you can eat in-store, and food is priced by weight. The clothing is also of a very high standard; look out for the sophisticated W Collection and local designer Stoned Cherrie.

SUPERMARKETS

Pick & Pay www.picknpay.co.za; **Shoprite** and **Checkers** www.shoprite.co.za; and **Spar** www.spar.co.za. These are the major supermarkets, and very large branches sell just about anything from washing-up liquid to wheelbarrows. For the budget-minded traveller, all have very good bakeries and deli counters serving hot and cold take-away meals. Pick & Pay also carries an affordable line of 'supermarket' clothing. Interestingly, Shoprite has over 800 supermarkets in 18 African countries. Some of the branches are open daily to 21.00. By law in South Africa, supermarkets can sell wine (though not on Sunday), but not beer or spirits. These can be found at bottle stores usually located next door to the supermarkets.

CLOTHES

Cape Union Mart www.capeunionmart.co.za. Here you will find everything you will need for the great outdoors, from tents and sleeping bags to hiking boots and compasses. There's also safari and sports clothes and shoes and luggage. Most of the gear is made by the company and is of top quality, and the staff are always very helpful.

Mr Price www.mrpricegroup.com. As the name suggests this is a cheap but fashionable brand especially popular with teenagers for the clothes, and young people setting up home for the first time for the good value homeware such as linen and bathroom accessories.

Truworths www.truworths.co.za; **Edgars** www.edgars.co.za; **Foschini** www.foshini.co.za; and **Stuttafords** www.stuttafords.co.za. These are all clothing department stores for both men and women. Stuttafords is at the top end with their own ranges and the international labels, whilst Edgars is cheap but keeps up with the trends and also carries international brands, such as Chip and Pepper jeans from Hollywood, and the US cosmetics line Bobby Brown. Truworths and Foschini are South Africa's answer to Top Shop. All also have cosmetic and skin care sections.

Young Designers' Emporium (YDE) www.yde.co.za. This is a unique concept and has been a huge success and there are now stores countrywide and in Dubai. Rails are 'rented' out, giving up to 40 fashion designers per shop the opportunity to sell and showcase their work under one roof. Whilst YDE have been approached by international designers they have decided to keep themselves totally South African.

BOOKS, MUSIC ETC

CD Wherehouse www.cdwherehouse.co.za. The best of the music chains, with a whole range of world and popular music, and the staff are very knowledgeable. There are especially good selections of African music and there is an entire room dedicated to classical and opera. They also sell music literature and autobiographies. Branches in Sandton City and the Zone@Rosebank stay open until 22.00.

CNA www.cna.co.za. This is a chain of large book, magazine and stationery stores, which also sells some CDs and DVDs, games and toys. The book selection is nowhere near as good as at Exclusive Books (see below), and they mostly sell popular bestselling novels, but they carry a good range of coffee table and souvenir books on Africa and just about every local and foreign magazine there is.

Exclusive Books www.exclusivebooks.co.za. This is the country's best bookshop, which usually has a coffee shop attached. Every kind of book imaginable is for sale here and it also carries an extensive range of foreign newspapers and magazines. If one branch doesn't have what you are looking for they will find the nearest branch that has. There are often book signings by authors at the Johannesburg branches and the January sales are legendary when the shops stay open until late. The biggest and best are in the Hyde Park and Sandton City malls.

Game www.game.co.za. These are very large hypermarkets selling everything imaginable with large toy and electronics sections. Items are often much cheaper here than elsewhere because of the enormous volume of stock they carry. *Game* are in the process of opening stores in other African countries such as Angola and Nigeria.

Glomail www.glomail.co.za. This chain of shops sells all those things you never realised you needed, and constantly reminds South Africans on the TV ads that these items are 'only available at Glomail'. They sell a lot of 'inventions' – revolutionary cookware, magical car polish, exercise contraptions that will make your stomach flat in 2 hrs, stuff that gets rid of acne in 20 mins, that sort of thing, and the staff are always on hand to demonstrate the gadgets. South Africans love this shop.

SHOPPING MALLS

Cresta Shopping Mall Beyers Naude Dr, Northcliff; ☎ 011 678 5306; www.crestashoppingcentre.co.za [2 B1] This is one of the city's largest malls and warrants a few hours for its good variety of shops. It features the chain stores but also a fair amount of individual shops. The car park is vast and there are lots of glass-fronted entrances. In the 26 years that it has been open it has had 8 refurbishments, but today looks like it's just recently been built. *Open Mon–Sat 09.00–18.00; Sun 09.00–14.00.*

Eastgate Shopping Centre Bradford Rd, Bedfordview; ☎ 011 616 2209; www.eastgatecentre.co.za [2 E2] Eastgate houses over 250 stores and most are large branches of the South African chains. It's set over 2 storeys, though the car park is a bit of a nightmare to get into with lots of tight corners and ramps. There's also the Burma Lake Flea Market nearby (see under *Flea markets*). *Open daily 09.00–17.00.*

Hyde Park Corner Jan Smuts Av, Hyde Park; ☎ 011 325 4340; www.hydeparkshopping.co.za [8 A1] This is in a good location in the heart of the northern suburbs off Jan Smuts and is considerably more upmarket than some of the other malls. There are 130 top-quality stores, many of which sell international brands, and there are some expensive designer clothes and jewellery boutiques. The cheaper chains don't feature. With many fine restaurants it's also a popular lunch spot for the surrounding affluent residents, as attested to by the rows of Mercs and BMWs in the car park. Woolworths is here, with an excellent array of goods including a good food section and café, and there's also an excellent branch of Exclusive Books. *Open Mon–Sat 09.00–17.00, Sun 10.00–14.00.*

Melrose Arch 32 Melrose Boulevard, off Corlett Dr, Melrose North; ☎ 011 684 0000; www.melrosearch.co.za [8 D1] Brand spanking new and very luxurious with a few upmarket boutique-type shops and many good-quality restaurants listed in the *Eating and Drinking* chapter — notably Moyo, one of the city's best restaurants. This is Johannesburg's newest and trendiest location for sidewalk eating and the architecture of the village-like enclosure is very modern and stylish. The complex also includes apartments and the Melrose Arch Hotel (see page 82). *Open daily 09.00–18.00.*

Oriental Plaza Main and Bree Sts, Fordsburg; ☎ 011 838 6752/3; www.orientalplaza-fordsburg.co.za [5 C6] The Oriental Plaza is not like the other modern super malls, but this is where locals go for the cheapest shopping around. It is run by Asians and whilst prices are fixed everything is negotiable. There are very many stores and shops selling cheap clothing, bedding, fabrics, curtains and household items mostly manufactured in Asia and China, and if you are patient and are prepared to rummage, you may come away with a few bargains, and once in a while genuine designer label clothing and shoes can be found. There's secure parking and you can pick up an Indian snack as you wander around to the strains of Bollywood pop music. *Open Mon–Thu 08.30–17.00, Fri 08.30–12.00, Sat 08.30–14.30.*

Sandton City corner Sandton Dr and Rivonia Rd, Sandton; ☏ 011 883 2011; www.sandtoncity.com; www.sandtonsquare.com; open daily 09.00–18.00 [7 C3] Johannesburg's best mall and one of the places to be seen in the city, as it's also home to many good restaurants and the impossibly upmarket shops around Nelson Mandela Square (see box). There is a full range of over 300 shops from the big chains to designer boutiques and this is where you would go if you wanted to buy a dress from *Versace*. There is also a VAT refund desk here for tourists to get their receipts stamped (see page 52) and a tourist office for *Gauteng Tourism*.

Southgate Mall corner Columbine and Rifle Range Rds, Mondeor; ☏ 011 942 1061 [2 B4] This is one of Johannesburg's largest malls — it's a huge cavernous concrete place and boasts nothing of interest architecturally. Nevertheless it has lots of shops at the cheaper end of the scale and has the largest concentration of furniture shops in the province. Given its position in the southwest of the city, it's very popular with the residents of Soweto. *Open daily 09.00–17.30.*

The Brightwater Commons corner Republic and Hans Strydom Rds, Randburg; ☏ 011 789 5052; www.brightwatercommons.co.za [1 C4] This used to be the Randberg Waterfront that opened in the mid 1990s

NELSON MANDELA SQUARE

Formerly the Sandton Square, the Nelson Mandela Square was renamed in 2004 when Mandela's eldest granddaughter unveiled a 6m bronze statue of the formidable man to celebrate ten years of democracy. It's a fine tribute to Mandela and the statue wears a broad smile; he's wearing one of his favourite baggy shirts, and he is doing the jiggy dance he is so famous for. It was sculpted by South African artists Jacob Maponyane and Kobus Hattingh, and from elbow to elbow is 2.3m across and weighs 2.5 tonnes. His shoes are a metre in length and it's rather delightful to watch small children sit on Mandela's feet! The square itself is a very attractive cobbled Italian-style piazza with fountains and it's beautifully lit up at night with twinkly lights. It is flanked by the Michelangelo Hotel, Michelangelo Towers, Raphael Penthouse Suites and Sandton Sun and Towers Intercontinental (see *Accommodation*, page 71 for details). Apart from the 93 luxurious shops it's also home to several first-class restaurants, art galleries, the Liberty Theatre on the Square and the Sandton Library. It's a wonderful spot to sit at an alfresco café and people-watch the glamorous and the wealthy as they swish by.

and the concrete mall surrounded a large artificial lake with lots of children's fairground rides around it. But for some reason it never became popular and over the years most of the major shops moved away leaving only cheap tacky shops and lots of empty units. In 2003 it was given a new image, most of the lake was filled in to form a grassy island, trees were planted and waterfalls developed. It looks a lot nicer and the shops, including Woolworths, are moving back in. There is a permanent flea market here and a music market selling CDs and DVDs. *Open Mon–Sat 09.00–17.00, Sun 09.00–13.00.*

The Mall of Rosebank and **The Zone@Rosebank** corner Cradock and Baker Rds, Rosebank; ✆ 011 788 5530; www.mallofrosebank.co.za [8 B3] This is one of the city's nicest malls as it's very open and the tree-lined avenues are pleasant to wander around. There's a good range of shops in the main mall though they tend to be more on the upmarket side and The Zone@Rosebank upstairs is very popular with teenagers and young people thanks to the cinema, bowling alley, trendy clothes shops and a very large CD shop. Both the African Craft Market and the Rosebank Rooftop Sunday Market are held here (see under *Flea markets* below). *Open Mon–Sat 09.00–17.00, Sun 10.00–14.00.*

Village Walk corner Maude St and Rivonia Rd, Sandown; ✆ 011 783 4620 [7 D2] The Village Walk is a small mall with a few shops, but it's best known for its wide variety of restaurants, bars and coffee shops, most of which have outdoor tables. The recommended restaurants including the excellent *Blues Room* are listed under *Entertainment and Nightlife*.

FLEA MARKETS

African Craft Market Rosebank Mall, Rosebank; ✆ 011 880 2906 [8 B3] A very good Sunday morning out is to go to one of the many restaurants with outside tables in Rosebank Mall for a big breakfast and a browse through the Sunday papers. Following this visit the African Craft Market and the Rosebank Rooftop Market on

Sunday (see below). At the craft market the former street traders have all been put under one roof and there are now over 140 stalls selling Johannesburg's best range of African art. There is frequent entertainment from singers and dancers dressed in traditional Zulu garb, and the traders are friendly and helpful. There is also a central point to pay for things by credit card. *Open daily 09.00–17.00.*

Bruma Lake Flea Market corner Ernest Oppenheimer and Marcia Av, Bruma; ✆ 011 622 9648 [2 E2] This is another extensive market, close to the Eastgate Shopping Centre, which attracts around one million visitors a year. The 620 stalls offer everything from clothes to crafts, and live entertainment can be enjoyed as you shop. There are African curios, secondhand clothing, antiques; in fact just about everything under the sun, and there are plenty of food stalls. *Open Tue–Sat 09.30–17.00.*

Bryanston Organic Market corner Bryanston and Culross Rds, Bryanston; ✆ 011 706 3671; www.bryanstonorganicmarket.co.za [1 C3] In 1976 a group of parents started this market to raise funds for a local school and today there are around 120 stalls specialising in organic products. For sale are a full range of all things made from nuts and grains and pulses, gluten-free items, dried fruit, teas, herbs, soya milk, vegetable juice and some wellness products and skin care items. In summer they hold occasional moonlight markets. Teas, cakes and light meals are available in the garden restaurant which has occasional live music. *Open Thu–Sat 09.00–15.00.*

Market Theatre Flea Market Newtown precinct, Bree St; ✆ 011 832 1641 [5 E6] This lively Saturday market held outside of the Market Theatre features a little bit of everything and is good for African curios whose vendors come from all over Africa. Bargain hard and you should get some good deals. *Open Sat 09.00–16.00.*

DOWNTOWN FASHION DISTRICT

One of the current developments of the inner city rejuvenation is the overhauling of the Fashion District, which covers several blocks between End and Von Wieligh streets, and Market and Kerk Streets in downtown Jo'burg. The area has been associated with the garment industry for over 50 years, but in the 1980–90s, along with the rest of the city, it went into decline. Today ongoing development and designation of the area as the Fashion District are encouraging South Africa's fashion industry to move back in and now many of the designers have their factories here. In 2003 the district got a facelift which included 'sewing patterns' being cut out of pavements and filled with mosaics, and current initiatives include tree planting and new signage. The Johannesburg Sewing Centre at 109 Pritchard Street is the biggest garment accessories supplier in Africa. It's not unusual for them to order a million metres of ribbon, they sell 7,000 styles of buttons, and dress patterns in six different languages – empowering more people to learn skills and set up their own businesses. They also run the SewAfrica Training Institute which has accreditation from the City & Guilds of London Art School, and which trains designers, tailors and seamstresses from all over Africa.

Panorama Flea Market Klip River Dr, Mulbarton; ✎ 011 682 2222; www.panoramafleamarket.com [2 D4] This market is good for families and there's something for everyone, including a children's playground, live entertainment from mostly Afrikaner singers, pony rides and a beer garden. There are 450 stalls selling a range of things. *Open Sat–Sun and public holidays 09.00–16.00.*

Rooftop Market Rosebank Mall, Rosebank; ☏ 011 442 4488 [8 B3] The Rooftop Market is regarded by many as South Africa's best flea market and it's popular with locals and tourists alike. Covering a large section of the mall's multi-storey car park, there are more than 500 stalls offering quality clothing, ceramics, art and craft objects, antiques and collectibles, secondhand books and there's a large food section selling cheap and tasty Thai, Chinese and Indian snacks and regular burgers and *borewors* rolls (local spicy sausage). Again there is a central point if you want to pay by credit card. *Open Sun and public holidays 09.30–17.00.*

9 Walks and Tours

CENTRAL JOHANNESBURG

If you have had no previous experience of walking around an African city, downtown Johannesburg is best visited on an organised tour. Although things are improving, it is not generally a good idea for tourists to wander casually around on foot. The city has a reputation for its high crime rate and danger of mugging at any time of the day or night. Around five years ago I was at the Carlton Centre and walked out onto the street where I was immediately pounced upon by several security guards who ushered me back inside and pointedly told me that it was not safe to walk the streets. Street life in Jo'burg was that hazardous. Today, the situation is a little better and the crime rate has come down, thanks mainly to better policing and the presence of CCTV cameras, but it has not wholly improved, so be on guard at all times if you do wander around the city centre, and keep valuables hidden – if you have to carry them at all. Also bear in mind that thousands of people go to work or go shopping in the CBD and the streets get very crowded.

If you do visit independently, stick to Braamfontein, Newtown and the main CBD around the western ends of President and Commissioner streets. Unless you are accompanied, do not walk around the eastern districts such as Doornfontein,

Hillbrow, Berea or Yeoville. It's also best to go on a weekday when everything is open and there are plenty of people around.

Nelson Mandela Bridge

From the northern suburbs the easiest approach to the city is over the fabulous new **Nelson Mandela Bridge** [5 E5], which goes from Bertha Street in Braamfontein to the newly named Ntemi Piliso Street (formerly West Street) in Newtown. The 284m-long steel-cable bridge with its distinctive white columns and blue lights has improved access to the city centre from the northern suburbs and is the newest feature on Jo'burg's skyline. Construction of the R38 million bridge – which spans 42 busy railway lines – started in September 2001 and it was opened in 2003 by Mandela two days after his 85th birthday. Across it run two lanes of traffic, two pavements and a cycle way. From the bridge, with Braamfontein behind you, you look west to the old **Newtown Railway Station** [5 E5] with its white and green ornate frame and roof. At present this stands derelict but the frame looks in good condition so hopefully it will be restored into something worthwhile in the future.

Starting at Newtown where you can park your car safely behind the Market Theatre, this walk starts at the Mary Fitzgerald Square, takes in the attractions of the Newtown precinct, some of the city centre's older buildings around Commissioner and Market streets, and ends on the 50th floor of the Carlton Centre. Although this tour starts in Newtown, there is also a car park at the Carlton Centre (and the Skyrink Car Park opposite on Main Street) so you could do it the other way around. The walk points out the historic sights and buildings and in between you'll have the opportunity to drink in the atmosphere of typical African street life – the thousands of people, blaring minibus taxis and chaotic traffic, small shops and hairdressers, and the informal hawkers and traders. Also notice the neat grid of streets, and the skyscrapers so tall you'll crane your neck looking skywards, and the more recent examples of the city's rejuvenation projects – the repaving of a street or square, the Metro Police decamped on a busy corner, or the new street signs or lights.

Newtown is located in the western sector of the Johannesburg CBD, covering an area that stretches from the marshalling yards and railway lines to the north, the M2 highway in the south, Ntemi Piliso Street to the east and Quinn Street to the west. At the turn of the 20th century, Newtown was originally known as Brickfields, simply because the area was rich in clay and brick-making was a popular local trade. As the land was close to the centre of early Johannesburg and the railway station, by 1896 it had attracted a number of immigrants who set up trading companies, brick companies and breweries, and many Indians set up shops and eateries along Locatie (now known as Carr Street), which led to the station. However in 1904, as a result of an outbreak of bubonic plague, the district was burned to the ground by the fire brigade. It was renamed Newtown and businesses began to re-establish themselves there. During the city's decline in the 1980–90s, Newtown became a dirty, overcrowded, dilapidated area filled with minibus taxis and overflowing street stalls, with piles of rubbish everywhere. The last few years the tide has completely turned with investment and improved security and the whole district has been revamped. It's now a very attractive and safe place to visit and there are a number of interesting things to see and do.

Newtown is dominated by the **Mary Fitzgerald Square** [5 E6] which was previously known as Aaron's Ground, and was originally a wagon site, but was used

MARY FITZGERALD

Mary Fitzgerald was born in Ireland in 1890, and later came to South Africa as a typist for the British Army. She first worked in the Castle in Cape Town before moving to Johannesburg as a typist for the Mine Workers' Union. She got drawn into the plight of the miners and by 1909 she was the only woman present at the Labour Party conference. She became a champion for women's rights, including women getting the vote, which they eventually did in 1930. During the tram workers' strike of 1911, she spoke at a protest meeting whilst holding a pick handle that was used by mounted police to break up the strike. The pick handle became her trademark, and she was known as pick-handle Mary. In 1921 she became the first woman on Johannesburg's City Council and in 1939 the square was named after her. She died in 1960 and there's a plaque commemorating her in Mary Fitzgerald Square.

for the many strikers' meetings in the early 20th century. In 2001 the newly paved square was reopened by President Thabo Mbeki. It can hold more than 50,000 people and will be a useful venue for events in the future; in 2005 the square hosted South Africa's version of the Live 8 global concerts. In the corner near the Market Theatre Complex is a giant TV screen that continually shows news and sport and attracts a large crowd if there's an important match on. This is reputedly the largest screen of its kind in Africa and measures $55m^2$. Also around the square are circular 'sky discs' showing the stellar constellations at various events such as the birth date of Mary Fitzgerald, the date of the first democratic election in 2004, and the date of the official re-launch of the square in 2001 on 16 December (which is the public holiday Reconciliation Day). The discs have optic-fibre lights that glow in the dark. If you come here in the evening, to visit one of the theatres or restaurants, notice how the square and Nelson Mandela Bridge are attractively lit up after dark.

All around the square and the neighbouring streets of Newtown are concrete plinths with carved wooden heads on top. Each carving is different and they are fashioned from old railway sleepers and represent a variety of Africa's cultural groups. To the northwest of the square notice the new **Brickfields** residential project on the block between Carr and Ntemi Piliso streets. Again this used to be a dilapidated area, but thanks to another city revitalisation project which was launched in 2005, 650 flats have been constructed for a range of income groups. They are reasonably attractive and built from bricks with some walls painted in bright primary colours, and again these were officially opened by President Mbeki. A fast-track planning approval system has been established by the local authorities to encourage more residential property development in the area.

Bree Street, on the north side of the square, is dominated by the imposing **Museum Africa** (see page 184 [5 E6]) which is housed in the city's old fruit and vegetable market. The vast building was completed in 1913 with a roof that is over 200m in length and it served as a produce market for more than 60 years. The museum displays the complex history of South Africa in an unconventional and thought-provoking manner, and it's well worth exploring for at least a couple of hours. To the right of the museum and at the end of the same building is the **Market Theatre Complex** (*open Mon–Sat 09.00–late, Sun 10.00–late* [5 E6]), which is also home to coffee shops, souvenir market traders, the famous **Gramadoelas** (see page 92 [5 E6]) restaurant and a branch of **Moyo** restaurant (see *Eating and Drinking*, page 96). The Market Theatre (see page 115) has withstood the test of time and remained in Newtown since it first opened its doors in 1976. It was started by a small group of dedicated actors who got together and raised the funds to save the grand old building and during refurbishment they did the actual physical labour themselves. The main entrance to the theatre is the grand Edwardian façade, which has three arched windows, flanked by twin domed towers. The main theatre is situated in the old Indian Produce Market, where some of the original vendors' signs still hang from the walls. From the 1970s the theatre made its name as a venue for anti-apartheid protest theatre. Today there are three venues at the theatre offering a varied programme of events.

On the precinct outside the theatre is **Kippies International Jazz Club** (*closed*). This building was rather incredulously modelled on an old-fashioned Edwardian toilet block, copied from the original toilets that once occupied a site 200m away which were built in 1913 at the same time as the old fruit and vegetable market. With its small arched windows and domed roof it was built in the 1980s and expanded in 1992, and the architect copied the toilet building so Kippies would fit in with the other old market buildings. The club was named after Kippie Morolong Moeketsi, a famous South African saxophonist, and until recently was for many years the top jazz venue in the country attracting a number of local and international artists. However, Kippies has recently and reluctantly been forced to close down because of structural problems (cracks in the walls and the roof). The building was initially condemned for demolition, but it was given a reprieve in early 2006 and awarded national heritage status for its importance to South African jazz, and a committee is presently deciding how to save the building and reopen the club. A few years ago the old potato sheds behind the Market Theatre Complex were converted into an arts centre focusing on the needs of children and young people, but it has been closed for some time so hopefully interest will be redeveloped for the venue.

On the opposite side of the square from the museum is a row of new shops and cafés and on the far right you'll see the office for **Gauteng Tourism** which has a few maps and leaflets to pick up (see page 30 [5 E6]). To the left of this row of shops is the entrance to the small **Newtown Park** [5 E6], which is now neat and tidy, with springy green grass and modern paved paths. There are two noteworthy modern art sculptures within the park – one of a pile of bright orange cars stacked up on one another, the other an abstract piece of blue and white triangles. On the right-hand side of the park is the **Bassline Club** (see page 119 [5 E6]), another one of Jo'burg's best venues for live jazz. Outside is a wonderful statue of an African female singer perched soulfully on a stool leaning into a microphone, with bare feet and long braided hair. You can sit on the empty stool next to her for a photograph. Next to Bassline is the **Dance Factory** [5 E6], which is a new practise venue for dance troupes that sometimes hosts live performances. On the adjacent side of the park is the **Workers Museum** (see page 190 [5 E6]), which showcases the role played by migrant workers in the early years of the city. It is set in a restored municipal workers compound, which once also served as the electricity department for the city. In the southeastern corner of the park is a small café where you can grab a cuppa, and the newly opened **Sci-Bono Discovery Centre** (page 187 [5 E6]) at the old Electric Workshop.

Walk through the car park at the south of the park that serves the Blue IQ office buildings, and cross President Street. Directly opposite the entrance to the car park and on the corner of President and the newly named Miriam Makeba streets (Bezuidenhout Street on older maps), in a big metal warehouse at 3 President Street, you will find the **Bus Factory** (page 175). On the opposite corner of President and Miriam Makeba streets are the **South African Breweries World of Beer** (see page 188 [5 E6]), and the **Horror Café** nightclub (see page 120 [5 E6]).

At the time of writing, the **Turbine Hall** on the corner of Jeppe and Miriam Makeba streets, a short walk to the north of the World of Beer, was being completely renovated and a new shopping centre was being built next door. This cavernous stone building was the home of Johannesburg's first coal-fired power station and was built in the 1920s, when it was considered to be the largest building under a concrete roof in the country and one of the finest examples of industrial architecture in the city. The four original cooling towers were demolished in 1985 and since then the Turbine Hall has been derelict and left to severely decay. Until recently it housed illegal squatters. However, once the renovations have been completed, and if funds can be raised, a decision has been made by the city council to move the **Johannesburg Art Galley** (see page 194 [6 G5]) into Turbine Hall over a three-year period. The gallery is currently located in a purpose-built building in Joubert Park, and the art collection has a rich history dating back to 1910. Despite opposition, the authorities believe moving it here would suit Newtown as the area is being promoted as a culturally rich district. Also the area around Joubert Park which borders the infamous suburb of Hillbrow is still in severe decline, with problems of theft and vandalism, and few people dare to venture there to visit the gallery. Time will tell if this move will take place and what Turbine Hall will become when it's finished. But if Johannesburg Art Gallery does move there, and because of the size and history of the building, the character of the development could be compared to that of Tate Modern in London.

To the west of here and running parallel between Pritchard and Jeepe streets, is the pedestrianised **Kirk Street Mall** [5 E6], where you will find all the usual chain shops that feature in all the shopping malls. A short walk up Jeepe Street and then along Ntemi Piliso Street and you will reach the new **Metro Mall** [5 E6]. This has replaced the old, chaotic and dirty minibus taxi rank and is now a sleek modern three-storey terminus for the taxis, which is also home to over 600 traders with market stalls. It is estimated that 150,000 commuters pass through it each weekday. The red-brick walls are covered with murals and there are various sculptures dotted around. It was built with the intention of not only tidying up the area, but to provide permanent homes for the informal traders that used to sell their wares at the side of the street. Inside it's a vibey place with hundreds of people moving through the buildings, going to and from work and home by way of the thousands of minibus taxis.

From here turn right off Bree into Sauer Street and you will reach the junction of Diagonal Street, which really is diagonal against the square grid of the city's streets. Here is a row of small unkempt shops where the shop owners have traded for decades. By contrast, opposite is the sleek blue-glass skyscraper that used to belong to the mining corporation De Beers, which is designed like a diamond with five facets, and next door the building that used to be Johannesburg's Stock Exchange in another modern high rise. The highlight of Diagonal Street is the **Museum of Man and Science** (*14 Diagonal St;* ☎ *011 856 4470* [5 E7]), though this is actually a shop: it's where *sangomas* (traditional healers) and their customers come to buy *muti* (herbs and traditional medicines). Above the door of the almost 70-year-old shop is a board proclaiming it as 'The King of Muti, Herbal and Homeopathic Remedies' and to the right of the door look out for the original 'non-whites' sign. Once inside be warned – the smell is very pungent, and in the darkened interior you are quite likely to bump your head against the various paraphernalia hanging from the ceiling – ostrich heads and feet, antelope horns, strings of seeds, hooves and tails, snake skins and various dried plants. On the counters are clay pots used by the *sangomas* to store their potions, walking and prayer sticks, drums, spears and shields. Also for sale are almost 2,000 types of herbs, plus bits of bark and branches, and rows of intriguing bottles of mixtures behind the counters. The shop claims it can serve all the tribes in Africa and all these strange bits and pieces have been collected from all over the continent. Tourists are welcome in the shop (and this is a mandatory stop on all city tours) and the more souvenir-like items for sale are for their benefit.

Around the corner from Diagonal Street, at 11a Kort Street, and easily missed as it's a tiny cramped place and up a shabby staircase between two shops, is **Kapitan's** [5 E7]. This is an Indian restaurant that was a favourite of Nelson Mandela when he was a young lawyer in the 1950s.

City Hall

From Diagonal Street head east along President Street and after a few blocks you will reach the **City Hall** [6 F6] which takes up a block between President and Market streets. The imposing building was built in 1915 and a further two storeys were added in 1937. While it was once home to the city council it was taken over by the Gauteng Legislature in 2001. The original building contractor was Mattheus Meischke, who also built the Meischke Building on the corner of Market and Harrison streets, housing the Guildhall Pub on its ground floor (see below). The architecture is typical of a British-style 19th-century town hall with classical columns, a portico and a high-domed tower. The original site was once the city's first **Market Square,** where perilously overloaded trestle tables sold produce amongst the muddy ruts of the wagon wheels in the early years. Later the square was grassed, trees were planted, fountains added and buildings went up on all sides. Today the remains of this square can be seen between the eastern entrance of the City Hall and the old **Post Office** [6 G6] on Rissik Street. The square, with its little park and two modern obelisks, has again been revitalised in 2003, and more recently the tarmac on Rissik Street has been ripped up and replaced with neat brickwork paving. Although the first postal agent in early Jo'burg was a canteen in the Ferreira's Camp where mail was stored in a gin box, the post office along with many other businesses in the city centre moved out in 1996 during the city's decline and the building has been empty since then its condition has rapidly deteriorated. This is a great tragedy as this is one of the oldest buildings in the city, built in 1897 and designed by President Paul Kruger's architect, Sytze Wierda, and at the time was the tallest building in town. It's a fine example of 19th-century civic architecture with four storeys of red-brick façade with arched windows, imposing clock tower and an ornate balcony that in the old days was used by the post master to throw mail down to the blacks who were not allowed inside the building. Its decay has not only been down to lack of maintenance but also due to vandalism and theft, and in the last decade, the clock hands and bells have been stolen from the clock tower, the copper dome on the roof has been peeled off, and the interior wooden balustrades, brass fittings, and original hardwood floorboards have been stripped. For the time being the building is boarded up, but a new security company is now in charge of looking after the building (the previous company is believed to have been behind the thefts from the building) and it's most certainly earmarked for rejuvenation, so hopefully restoration will start soon. It's a fine building with a lot of character, and, thankfully unlike other properties in downtown Jo'burg, it has not been occupied by squatters, who in turn cause further decay and instability to properties such as this.

To the south of the City Hall on the corner of Harrison and Market streets is the historic **Guildhall Pub** (☏ 011 836 5560; *open daily Mon–Fri 11.00–late; Sat 11.00–19.00* [6 F6]). The original one-storey building was built in 1888 soon after gold was discovered and served the early miners. Within ten years a second storey was added and then in 1913 another four were added, built by Mattheus Meischke, who also built the City Hall, and the building became known as the Meischke Building. The pub remained open during the 1980–90s, though was little more than an informal and scruffy *shebeen* until 2003. Since then, new owners have restored it to its former glory.

Two blocks south of the pub and City Hall on the corner of Fox and Loveday streets is the **Rand Club** (☏ 011 834 8311; *www.randclub.co.za* [6 F7]), Johannesburg's original gentlemen's club that once served the wealthy mining magnates in the formative years of the city, though it permitted membership to women in 1993. The neo-Baroque-style building was erected in 1904 and it was South Africa's most famous imperialist,

Cecil John Rhodes, who decided on the club's location. He is said to have walked up Commissioner Street a few years earlier and looked upon the bare veld which is now Loveday Street, and said 'Here we must have a club'. Rhodes donated some of the money to build the club and in the club's Rhodes Room is a life-sized portrait of him. The lovely four-storey building with its grand columns, galleries and sweeping staircases, and imposing lobby with a domed stained-glass windowed roof, has several dining rooms and bars, libraries and billiard rooms, and offices are let out in the upstairs rooms. At the time of great wealth in early Johannesburg, it was furnished with great opulence to resemble an English club and the entrance hall is said to be modelled on that of the Reform Club in London. The walls are lined with dozens of portraits of men who have been part of the city's history, including more recent ones of President Mbeki and Mandela, and the rooms are decorated with antique furniture, sweeping drapes, Persian rugs, original Punch cartoons, hunting paraphernalia and chandeliers. Sadly, there was a damaging fire at the club in June 2005 and some of the pictures and other valuables were lost, and it was closed for almost a year. However, at the time of writing it had just been reopened after extensive refurbishment. Non-members cannot go in without an invitation, but there's no reason that you cannot ask at reception if you can look inside.

A short walk along Fox Street and you will reach **Ghandhi Square** [6 G7], the main terminus in the city for the metro buses. This has recently been re-laid with mosaic brickwork around a traffic circle and four lanes of bus stops. A statue of Mahatma Ghandhi sits to the side of the traffic circle in his lawyer's flowing cloak and

Ghandhi Square

carrying a law book. The father of India's struggle for independence from Britain, his philosophy of passive resistance was first adopted in South Africa in the struggle against racial segregation against Indians. He lived in and practised law in Johannesburg from 1903 to 1913, and from 1906 became active in politics after (amongst other events) being thrown off a train at Pietermaritzburg for sitting in a white carriage. In 1906 laws proposed that Indians and Chinese were to register their presence, give fingerprints and carry pass books. A protest meeting was organised and Ghandhi spoke to the protesters following the theme 'violence begets violence' to encourage a peaceful march through Johannesburg. Despite its peaceful nature, the marchers were arrested and thrown into prison at the Old Fort (see page 175), a place Ghandhi was to spend another four sentences over the coming years in his resistance of Indians carrying pass books. The square is on the site of the city's first courthouse in the area, where he had his legal practice, and was renamed Ghandhi Square in 1999. A series of information panels around the square tell the story of Ghandhi's connection to the city.

If you continue along Main or Fox street for four blocks you'll reach the **Carlton Centre** [6 G7] and the Carlton Hotel (currently closed) which take up the block between Main and Commissioner Streets. Opened in 1973, the 50-floor Carlton

Centre is South Africa's tallest building at 223m, and the 600-roomed hotel at its feet was once the city's premier five-star hotel. Henry Kissinger, François Mitterrand, Hillary Clinton, Margaret Thatcher, Whitney Houston and Mick Jagger were among the hotel's more revered guests during its 25-year history. Then, the rot set in, most of the office tenants in the centre moved out and in 1997 the hotel shut down. The lavish furniture and fittings were sold off to furnish hotels and restaurants at Gold Reef City. Today things have improved and most of the offices in the Carlton Centre are leased out and the shops have moved back into the now-popular Carlton Mall at the base of the tower. The hotel is still closed but it's likely to reopen again in the future as investment into the city centre grows.

On the ground floors of the Carlton Centre is the shopping mall and cinema complex spread with all the usual shops and a food court. On the second floor is the entrance to the **Top Of Africa** (08.00–19.00; R7.50 adults, R3.50 children under 12), a 50-storey elevator ride to a glassed indoor viewing floor. The lift takes an impressive 35 seconds to reach the top and you may feel your ears pop on the way up and down. On all sides of the viewing floor are large windows, some floor to ceiling, and from here is the best view of Johannesburg there is; you can look directly down at the various rooftops of office buildings and apartment blocks in various states of repair and use. To the north are the forested hills of the northern suburbs in the distance, with the vast railway yards, Newtown and the Nelson Mandela Bridge in the foreground. To the northeast are the dense crop of Hillbrow's apartment tower blocks, including the giant circular **Ponte City** (see box, page 158

Ponte City [4 J4], at 173m high, is the tallest residential building in Africa and has 470 flats. The most striking feature on the city's skyline, with its huge flashing Vodacom advertisement on the roof, it has become the unofficial landmark of Johannesburg. Located in Hillbrow, the enormous 54-storey tower is actually a cylinder and the open inner core was built to ensure that every room had access to natural light. It was built in 1975, when Hillbrow was a largely white, middle-class neighbourhood especially favoured by pensioners. But when these residents started to move out in the 1980s as conditions in Hillbrow deteriorated, immigrants from mainly west Africa began to move in, and Ponte soon became a ghetto inhabited by a criminal element. However a new management company took over in

[4 J4]) and the **Hillbrow Tower** [4 H3], a telecommunications tower which belongs to Telkom and which at 270m is the tallest structure (with a lift) in Africa. To the west are views of the heart of the CBD, where President and Commissioner streets head west in straight lines with the minibus taxis snaking through the intersections, and you can clearly see Ghandhi Square and the various other busy taxi and bus stands. Looking south, notice how the skyscrapers suddenly stop short a few blocks south of Commissioner Street. This is because this area was where the gold-mine tunnels ran underneath the city, making the ground highly unstable for high-rise construction. Instead there are the low lying industrial areas spread out to the south

2000, installed a sophisticated security system and spent millions of rand on improvements and maintenance, including replacing the 1970s furnishings. One of the biggest projects for the company was removing the three storeys of garbage filling the base of the cylinder – accumulated since the first tenants moved in over 25 years earlier – and getting the lifts working again, which had all fallen into disuse (in a 54-storey building!). The flats are now also promoted to students and families and these days there is less of a criminal element living at Ponte City. One sad peculiarity about the building is that it has the highest number of suicide-related falling deaths of any building in the world. The majority of jumpers jumped outwards, off the edge of the building, rather than inwards or down into the cylinder.

and the west, intercepted by flyovers, railway lines and, ubiquitous in Johannesburg, the mine dumps. These used to be unsightly, grey dusty heaps, but these days most have been planted with trees, and grass has been cultivated to make them blend naturally with the environment. From here you can also see the roofs of the 65,000m² **Johannesburg Fresh Produce Market** in City Deep which is the largest of its kind in Africa and South Africa's biggest distribution centre for fruit and vegetables. It attracts up to 45,000 buyers a day from all the southern African countries. The viewing floor has a comfortable café and bar where you can grab a drink before catching the lift back down.

Soweto (short for South West Township) is a sprawling township, or, more accurately, a cluster of townships and suburbs to the southwest of Johannesburg. It was the centre of political campaigns during the struggle against apartheid, including the 1976 Soweto Uprising, so therefore most of the sights have political and historical significance (for a full history of Soweto, see page 7). It is estimated that Soweto is home to a (nearly wholly black) population of 900,000 and the suburbs represent a mixture of housing to reflect different socio-economic groups, as in any city. There are the original grey, four-roomed dwellings built from the 1930s in areas such as Diepkloof, and also the smart newer suburbs such as Dube, housing the middle-class blacks with schools and playgrounds and tarred roads. These days buying a cappuccino or a BMW in Soweto is not a problem and Soweto is reportedly home to over 20 millionaires. However, there are also the hostels – monstrous, prison-like buildings, originally built for male migrant miners, and although more recently the government has converted some of these into family flats they still remain unattractive. And at the edge of Soweto are the rudimentary squatter camps or informal settlements, usually the homes of unemployed people who make their shacks from sheets of corrugated iron and planks of wood which are freezing in winter and scorching hot in summer. These areas lack amenities like running water and electricity and are a hazard to live in. However, the shacks represent real homes and there is a great sense of community; the government is on a constant programme to rehouse shack dwellers into proper houses.

It's easy enough to drive yourself to Soweto these days, and most of the attractions such as the Hector Pieterson Museum (see page 179), Mandela Family Museum (see page 183), Desmond Tutu's house and church, Walter Sisulu's house and Orlando West High School are all clumped together within walking distance of each other in Orlando West. Long gone are the days when white people stood out like sore thumbs, and in fact over 200,000 tourists visit Soweto each year. In 2006 the US reality TV show *The Amazing Race* staged its activities in Soweto, one of which involved taking a terrifying walk across a very narrow slatted bridge slung between the abandoned Orlando cooling towers. Going by yourself, however, means you will miss out on being with a guide who will tell you all the stories and history of Soweto. Tourism has been very important for Soweto for the last decade and most guides are Soweto residents and the tours are informative and fun. A half-day tour costs in the region of R250–350 and for a list of tour operators see page 68. Most tours will take you through each of the different suburbs to show you both the affluent and impoverished aspects of Soweto, and will perhaps include a visit to an informal township, minibus taxi stand or market. They will certainly allow time to visit the new Hector Pieterson Museum and the Mandela Family Museum (see page 170) and show you the sights such as Archbishop Tutu's house, Orlando Stadium and the Baragwanath Hospital [2 B4]. The latter is on Old Potchefstroom Road and is the largest hospital in Africa, where most of Soweto's population was born. It used to be a military hospital but was turned into a public hospital in the 1940s. Today it is the biggest teaching hospital in the world with about 3,000 beds, and it specialises in trauma and AIDS research, which attracts a lot of overseas students. Next to it is a footbridge over the road and if you climb up here there are good views of Soweto sprawling away in every direction. Nearby to the footbridge, notice the traffic lights (robots in South Africa) that have an HIV sign in the amber light, and an AIDS sign in the red light. Very symbolic. Across Old Potchefstroom Road are the Baragwanath taxi rank and market and the Baragwanath Mall on the corner of Nicholas Street. Take the road to the left of the mall and after a few hundred metres you'll reach the old abandoned Orlando power station [2 A4] and the two distinctive cooling towers – one painted blue and white to advertise the First National Bank, the other painted in a marvellous cartoon image of famous Soweto landmarks, and scenes and images from everyday life, like taxis and street vendors, and people's heroes such as Nelson Mandela. There are plans for much redevelopment in this area, including turning the power station into a giant shopping mall, extensive housing projects including lakeside flats (a first for Soweto), and there are even rumours of constructing viewing platforms at the top of the cooling towers, and making them a destination for extreme sports such as abseiling, base jumping and the world's first indoor bungee jump!

Other sights in Soweto include the **Regina Mundi Catholic Church** further down Old Potchefstroom Road. It is a rather ordinary-looking 1960s construction, but one that still bears scars from the 1976 Soweto Uprising, when police stormed through its doors firing live ammunition at fleeing schoolchildren. There are still bullet holes in the ceiling. Outside is an attractive park with fountains and green lawns and memorials and plaques representing the church's place in history. Some of the Truth and Reconciliation Commission hearings, presided over by Archbishop Desmond Tutu, took place in the church in the late 1990s. There's also a more delightful story attached to the church. In 1998 it was visited by the then president of the US Bill Clinton and his wife Hillary. Firstly they caused uproar in the press by taking Holy Communion during the Catholic service they attended (Bill is a Baptist and Hillary a Methodist), and then to top it all the priest based his sermon on adultery at the time when Clinton was embroiled in the Monica Lewinsky scandal. The press reported that Clinton looked 'visibly uncomfortable'.

WALTER SISULU SQUARE OF INDEPENDENCE *off Union Rd, Kliptown;* ☏ *011 945 3111; www.joburgtourism.com; open Mon–Fri 08.00–17.00. There is a new branch of the Johannesburg Tourism Company at the square called the Soweto Tourism Information Centre. In time it will house a restaurant and internet café, but for now look out for the wonderful display of photography of Soweto amongst other artwork.*
The Walter Sisulu Square of Independence in Kliptown, formerly Freedom Square, was the site of the 'Congress of the People' on 26 June 1955, which was attended by 2,884 delegates from a broad alliance of various political groups, and 7,000 spectators. Their demands for a free and democratic South Africa were incorporated into the Freedom Charter, which was adopted at the congress. Here delegates drew up a new vision for the country based on thousands of submissions collected by volunteers all over the country. The police broke up the gathering and

arrested many leaders, but nevertheless the Freedom Charter became the backbone of ANC politics, and the new constitution of 1996 was based largely on its rights-for-all sentiments. These were the original 1955 pledges: The people shall govern; all national groups shall have equal rights; the people shall share in the country's wealth; the land shall be shared among those who work it; all shall be equal before the law; all shall enjoy equal human rights; there shall be work and security; the doors of learning and culture shall be opened; there shall be houses, security and comfort; there shall be peace and friendship. Walter Sisulu was a delegate at the congress, a major figure in the anti-apartheid struggle, deputy president of the ANC and like Mandela was sent to jail after being tried in the Rivonia Treason Trials. The Freedom Square was renamed the Walter Sisulu Square of Independence in his honour after his death in 2003. Back in the 1950s it was just a dusty square, but since 2003 it has been modernised as a memorial and tourist attraction and it has recently been declared a National Heritage Site. The complex consists of two long, narrow buildings encompassing the square, with ten giant concrete slabs on the eastern edge representing the ten clauses of the Freedom Charter. At the time of writing the buildings had only just been completed and small shops were moving in. The former informal market has been incorporated along one side in a semi-open concrete enclosure where traders have individual lock-up storage containers for their goods. A Kliptown Museum is presently being discussed. At the northern end is a tall conical tower made from red bricks which is the Freedom Charter Monument. During the 2005 50th anniversary of the signing of the Freedom Charter, President Mbeki lit the Flame of Freedom in the tower.

Kliptown was made up predominantly of informal settlements which surrounded the square on all sides. Part of the R300 million development of the square was to re-house the shack dwellers and now new houses are presently being built all over Kliptown. Notice the railway line that runs along the southern side of the square – the famous Blue Train and other luxurious trains run through Soweto on this line.

ALEXANDRA *For more information visit www.alexandra.co.za.*

Established in 1912, Alexandra is one of the earliest urban black settlements in Jo'burg, pre-dating even Soweto: it recently celebrated its 90th birthday. It's the only township in the northern suburbs, located between Sandton and the airport. For decades it was mostly made up of shacks packed as densely as playing cards but in the last few years it has been the site of a multi-million rand presidential development initiative. Like Soweto you can visit on a tour through one of the operators listed on page 68.

The land was originally a farm owned by a Mr Papenfus who named it after his wife Alexandra, and by 1912 it had been proclaimed as a black township. During apartheid some 50,000 people were forcibly removed to Soweto and other designated areas, although it was never the intention to remove Alexandra altogether as it was home to an important labour force to Johannesburg's northern suburbs. During apartheid one of the more famous incidents that happened in Alex (as it is affectionately called) was the bus boycott that took place in the 1940s because the city wanted to increase the fourpenny fare to five pennies (one penny is around R1 in today's terms). The township came out in protest, and for six months residents walked to and from Alexandra to work in town along Louis Botha Avenue, a distance of up to 15km. This was the first sign that street-based political movement and protest could grow. In 1956 there were protests by women against the extension of the pass laws to women. A number were arrested and were sent to the women's section of the infamous Number Four jail where they were kept in appalling conditions. When the women were released they refused to leave the prison until water was splashed on them with hosepipes; to flush them out of the prison. See page 175 for information about the prison which is now a museum. During the 1976 Soweto Uprising violent protest spread to Alex where 19 people died, and in February 1986 a violent uprising called the 'Alex Six Days' occurred in which 40 people were killed. In the early 1990s violence broke out between men living in the hostels and local residents and for a time the area around the hostels was dubbed Beirut.

Today Alex is witnessing much building and gradually houses are replacing the shacks. In 1999, an athlete's village was built for the All Africa Games on the Far East Bank with 1,700 semi-detached units, and now these are occupied by Alexandra residents. In 2001 President Mbeki announced the Alexandra Renewal Project. So far 7,000 people have been moved from the riverbanks where once the shacks teetered dangerously on steep slopes, and these banks have now been reinforced and grassed. Almost 14,000 houses will have been built by 2008, 3,000 trees have been planted, sewers are being laid, and a new police station has been built to help to reduce crime. Tours cover historical buildings, shanty town areas, Mandela's old house (he lived in Alex briefly in the 1940s), the Roman Catholic Church, a hostel, new developments of the Alex Renewal Project and the smarter East Bank over the Jukskei River.

PARKTOWN

The Parktown and Westcliff Heritage Trust organises walking tours through Parktown on Saturday afternoons; ☏ *011 482 3349; www.parktownheritage.co.za.* [3 E2]
The suburb of Parktown just to the northeast of the city centre and accessed off the M1 is the oldest residential suburb in Johannesburg and is home to some turn-of-the-20th-century architecture. Despite its proximity to Hillbrow (on the other side of Empire Road) it has retained its peaceful, leafy atmosphere and is the location of many fine mansions, including some built by the renowned architect Sir Herbert Baker. In 1892 Florence Phillips rode north from the dusty, noisy, mining town that was early Johannesburg, and when she reached the first crest she saw the open veld stretching to the Magaliesberg Mountains in the distance. She persuaded her husband to build her a mansion where the Johannesburg Hospital stands today and the Phillips were soon joined by other successful entrepreneurs.

The legacy is Parktown's Victorian mansions, English Edwardian villas, and the stone houses of Sir Herbert Baker, including his own home, the Stone House.

Sir Herbert Baker was born in 1862 in Britain and trained at the Royal Academy and Architectural Association before arriving in South Africa in 1892. He was commissioned by Cecil John Rhodes, who sent him to Italy, Greece and Egypt to study the classical styles of these countries in order to incorporate them into the grand buildings he wished to see erected in South Africa. He first designed and built houses and churches in the Cape for which he incorporated local stone, thatch and timber, before moving to Johannesburg where he built many fine buildings, including schools, churches and a number of Parktown mansions. All these buildings were built with locally quarried stone and the houses were known for their stateliness and clean lines. His most famous building is probably the Union Building in Pretoria.

The tour takes about three hours and covers several Herbert Baker houses and gardens. These include Pilrig House at 1 Rockridge Road, a classic Baker house with a stone and mortar base up to the first level, and an inviting veranda with white pillars. Next door is St Margaret's, also a Baker house, built in 1905 and surrounded by a stunning garden. The driveway has three old oak trees marking its entrance, and charming old lamps on either side of the gate posts. The house is now owned by a German investment bank and has been beautifully restored and maintained. Also on Rockridge Rd is Baker's own house, Stone House, the first house he built in Parktown. The front entrance is an impressive arched wooden door, with a white-pillared atrium behind and above the door, linking the west and east wings of the house. Again the garden is lovely and full of trees. When Baker was building these houses, the landscape was completely barren, without a tree in sight. Parktown is another area of the city that reminds us that Johannesburg is one of the largest manmade forests in the world.

10 Museums and Sightseeing

MUSEUMS

If you only have time to visit one museum in Johannesburg make it the superb Apartheid Museum (see page 172). In addition to the range of museums listed here, there are several in Soweto (see below).

ABSA GROUP MUSEUM *187 Fox St, city centre;* ☏ *011 350 4167; open Mon–Fri 08.00–16.00; free.* [6 H6]
The ABSA Group (one of the country's leading banks) Museum is dedicated to the history of South Africa's ABSA and money. It houses the largest collection of South African currency in the world and also older, non-paper currencies such as cowry shells and Venetian glass beads used in older times. There are also old coins which were found on sunken ships off South Africa's coast, 600 old money boxes, and displays on bank-related crime and how to use an ATM. It's mostly geared towards children, and ABSA is doing a fair amount in the country to promote maths amongst young people.

ADLER MUSEUM OF MEDICINE *In the foyer of the university's Medical School, 7 York Road, Parktown;* ☏ *011 717 208; open Mon–Fri 09.30–16.00.* [4 G2]

SECRET SAFARI

From 1986 to 1993, *Africa Hinterland Safaris*, a bogus company set up in London by sympathisers of the ANC, carried over 500 innocent passengers on overland trips from Kenya to South Africa on a trip of a lifetime. However the passengers were unwitting participants in an ANC weapons smuggling operation. On each trip, when the truck got to Lusaka, Zambia, the crew would leave the passengers at the campsite and go to a secret location where they would load one tonne of ammunition into the truck and hide it in a space between the seats and the lockers on the side of the truck; effectively the passengers were unknowingly sitting on top of the guns. They then drove into South Africa where the truck offloaded the passengers in Johannesburg and the ammunition in Durban. They did this 40 times and never got caught. There is a wonderful documentary about this called *Secret Safari*, with some reconstruction footage and interviews with everyone involved. The filmmakers also tracked down some of the ex-passengers to tell them the story. Some were appalled that they had been used in such a way, but most were simply completely gob-smacked.

This private collection of medical and pharmaceutical memorabilia was started by Dr Adler in 1962. Today there are over 40,000 objects from stethoscopes to dental chairs. There are superbly authentic mock-ups from early Johannesburg of a doctor's rooms, a dentist's, an optician's and a pharmacy with its gleaming mahogany and glass cabinets stuffed to the gills with remedies. There is also a display on African traditional medicine which explains the role of the *sangoma* (traditional healer) in African societies, plus a look at alternative medicine such as acupuncture.

APARTHEID MUSEUM *corner Northern Parkway and Gold Reef Rd, Ormonde;* ↘ *011 496 1822; www.apartheidmuseum.org; open Tue–Sun, 10.00–17.00; R25 adults, R12 children and senior citizens.* [2 C3]

The Apartheid Museum is the best museum I have ever visited and the emotions it evokes are quite remarkable, whatever the extent of your knowledge about the apartheid era. It has been critically acclaimed throughout the world and is a must on any visit to South Africa. It takes visitors on an emotional but informative journey from the year apartheid was instigated in 1948 to when Nelson Mandela became president in 1994, and easily demonstrates the triumph of human spirit over adversity through the series of exhibitions. The museum opened in 2001 and was (naturally) officially opened by Mandela himself. A team of filmmakers, historians and architects have created a dramatic and moving experience for visitors, and the whole story of apartheid is told from the moment you purchase your ticket. These are plastic cards indicating 'white' or 'non-white' and specifically refer to the pass laws that segregated the

Apartheid Museum

races. Tickets are issued at random, and visitors get to go through one of two entrances into the museum where there are exhibits of pass books for each category. The building itself is very stark, with lots of barbed wire, bare brick, steel and harsh concrete – there could be no better environment to showcase its subject.

Once inside you go through a series of 'spaces' dedicated to the apartheid planners, pass laws, enforced relocation, early protests in the townships, the rise of the ANC and other black opposition groups, the 1976 Soweto Uprising and Sharpeville Massacre, and the political incarcerations and executions that occurred during apartheid. In this particular space are 121 nooses hanging from the ceiling – one for each of the 121 political executions. The spaces move on to the 1980–90's protests and reforms, right through to Mandela's release, the 1994 elections and the drafting of a new constitution that granted equal rights to all of South Africa's citizens. Some of the more evocative displays are of the footage of police vehicles driving through the townships which can be viewed from inside a *Casspir* (an armoured tank-like vehicle used by the police in the townships during apartheid) and photographs taken by Ernest Cole of the townships in the 1960s. These are tragic but beautiful images and, as a white photographer, he managed to get himself classed as coloured so he could enter the townships to take the pictures.

All over the museum are several hundred TV screens showing footage of the apartheid regime, and most of the story is demonstrated on television. It's interesting to note that South Africa did not start broadcasting television until the mid 1970s, and even then the authorities were unlikely to allow TV companies to record civil strife against the establishment. This footage has been collected from news stations all over the world, and clearly demonstrates that not only did the breakdown of apartheid come about by the black protest element within the country, but by international pressure as a result of these images. It could be argued that television played a part in the struggle against apartheid, as it has for other conflicts in modern history: Vietnam, the Biafran War, the Gulf conflict and Iraq. The footage shows everything from the building of Afrikaner nationalism and life in the townships, to black and white resistance and celebrated speeches and moving tributes from South Africa's champions who beat the apartheid system. South African visitors are invited to leave their own historical artefacts – pass books or photographs for example – and record their experiences under apartheid on video tape. Highly recommended, and who would have thought that a museum could showcase history that is only just over a decade old. I like the museum's tourist literature that says 'The reason people wouldn't visit our country is now our biggest tourist attraction'. On a final note, it's very balanced politically speaking – a staunch conservative Afrikaner from a *dorp* in the Free State, to a Soweto schoolchild, to a tourist who has little knowledge of what happened to South Africa in the 20th century, will come away very much wiser and much rewarded.

BERNARD PRICE INSTITUTE FOR PALAEONTOLOGICAL RESEARCH (also known as the James Kitching Gallery); *Van Riet Lowe Building, corner Jorissen St and Yale Rd, East Campus, Wits University;* ✆ *011 716 2727; open Mon–Fri 08.30–16.00.* [3 E4]

This is the largest fossil collection in the southern hemisphere. Many exhibits have been collected from the Sterkfontein Caves (see page 215), as well as other regions of Africa. As Ross from *Friends* would know, the fossils are technically referred to as a palaeontological display and the stars of the show are Fred and Fang, two life-sized dinosaurs that have been reconstructed from fossils. These have huge fangs and as they are robotic are rather frightening-looking.

BLELOCH GEOLOGICAL MUSEUM *Geosciences Building, East Campus, Wits University;* ☎ *011 717 6665; open Mon–Fri 08.00–16.30; R8.* [3 E4]
As you would expect from a geological museum this houses a collection of rocks and minerals to demonstrate different aspects of geology. It's mostly aimed at school groups and there are simple displays showing the earth's crust and topography and similar subjects.

BUS FACTORY *3 President St; open Mon–Fri 09.00–17.00, Sat 10.00–14.00.* [5 E6]
This is a permanent craft exhibition of objects from around the country and there is one old double-decker bus on display. At present there are only a few exhibits, which look a bit lost in the big open space, so again hopefully this venue will improve. It's located in what was a bus mechanics' depot built in the 1930s.

CONSTITUTION HILL MUSEUM *corner Kotze and Hospital Sts, Braamfontein;* ☎ *011 274 5300; open Mon–Fri 09.00–17.00 (last ticket 16.00), Sat–Sun 09.00–12.00; R15* *adults, R10 senior citizens, R5 children under 12, free entry on Tue. The 1¹/₂hr tours leave from the visitors' centre on the hour, or you can walk around by yourself. There's a coffee shop and museum shop and full wheelchair access with slopes and lifts. [4 G4]*

Constitution Hill is the site of Johannesburg's notorious Old Fort prison complex, commonly known as Number Four, which has now become a major tourist attraction and was opened in March 2004. For decades, thousands of prisoners passed through the complex, men and women, and were held in dirty, overcrowded conditions. Its reputation reached its peak during the apartheid era when as many as 2,000–3,000 people a day passed through the prison, mostly being arrested and imprisoned for a day or two for not carrying their pass books. The story goes that if an employee didn't turn up for work, the employer would phone Number Four to see if he or she was there. Originally built in 1904, conditions were thought to be the worst in the country and Number Four instilled fear and horror in the minds of most black people. The prison was only closed in 1983. The museum's curator Kwena Mokwena said in 2003, 'When I was a kid growing up in Soweto, guys who'd been in Number Four were revered for having survived'. Up to 60 black prisoners were held in cells designed for 20, simple porridge was dished out on plates that were never washed, blankets were full of lice, and violent gang leaders ruled the roost. Meanwhile white prisoners shared two-bunk cells and were given considerably better food. Today the old prison cells have been converted into an interactive museum with another state-of-the-art TV system that shows footage of former prisoners recounting their experiences. Famous inmates include Mahatma Ghandhi and Nelson Mandela, and most of the other leading activists during the struggle against apartheid ended up at Number Four at some point over the decades.

There are three entrances to the complex: on Sam Hancock St (visitors' entrance) which takes you up the Great African Steps, which is a walkway symbolising the journey between the past and future with the walls of the old prison on one side and the glass walls of Constitutional Court (see below) on the other; on Kotze St (schools entrance) through the gate and tunnel of the original Old Fort; and on Hospital Extension St (for visitors with special needs and large tour buses). After paying for entry at the visitors' centre you can join the tour or wander around the old cells, still with their peeling walls and graffiti on the back of the doors, to see the exhibits that explain how appallingly the prisoners were treated in this notorious complex, which gives a harrowing insight into what it was like to be a black prisoner during the dark days of apartheid. Looking into the isolation cells, or dark pits as they were known, it's easy to imagine how horrific this place once was. Other exhibits include a flogging frame, wardens' batons, and the tin pots still encrusted with porridge that the prisoners ate from. The Old Fort part of the complex, not really a fort but a rampart enclosing the prison buildings, is where the white prisoners were kept in considerably better conditions, though at one time Nelson Mandela was also kept here on the hospital wing, not for need of medical attention, but so the guards could keep a better eye on him. Conditions in the adjoining women's prison were supposedly a little better, but nevertheless the black women were kept together whilst the white women (many of them activists) each had their own cell. Some of the Hillbrow high rises overlook the complex and it is said that residents could watch the prisoners in the exercise yard from their lofty apartments.

The complex is now also the location of the highest court in South Africa, the Constitutional Court, built in 2002. Part of the prison (the awaiting trial block) was torn down to make way for the new courthouse, and with an innovative idea of symbolism, 150,000 of the old bricks from the awaiting trial block have been re-used in the new court, demonstrating injustice of the past being part of justice in the future. Two of the stairwells of the old prison have been preserved and are incorporated into the design of the new building. On the logo of the court is a tree under which people are in discussion. This is also represented in the lobby of the court where the pillars are askew, to represent tree trunks and branches; natural light comes through the ceiling, and lights are arranged like leaves. Overall the building is cleverly designed with lots of timber, black slate and steel, and steps lead down the Constitutional Square at the front. This is also the home of the largest human rights library in the southern hemisphere.

The Constitutional Court was established in 1994 after the democratic elections. Each of the 11 justices are independent and impartial and are not permitted to be members of parliament, government or political parties. They are chosen by the president and are expected to hold a 12-year term. The court represents the country's supreme law and sits in judgement if the regular legislature declares a law that may be unconstitutional. Public attendance is allowed and you can creep into the back of the court room and sit in the public gallery if court is in session. For more information visit www.concourt.gov.za.

Also nearby to Constitution Hill in this region of Braamfontein is the **Miner's Monument** [4 F4] which is located in the middle of the roundabout (or traffic circle in South Africa), at the top of Rissik Street. The bronze statue was erected in the city in 1964 by the Chamber of Mines and depicts three large miners in shorts, gumboots and hard hats holding a giant drill. A few years ago thieves stole one of the giant boots, presumably to sell off for scrap metal, but this has since been replaced by a new boot. To the northeast of here on Loveday Street is the **Civic Theatre** (see page 114 [4 F4]), a rather ugly concrete structure built in the 1960s, but it's nevertheless a good venue for theatre and there is also a branch of **News Café** here (see page 108).

HECTOR PIETERSON MUSEUM AND MEMORIAL *corner Khumalo and Pela Sts, Orlando West, Soweto; 011 536 0611; open Mon–Sat 10.00–1700; Sun 10.00–16.30; R10 pp. There is an excellent bookshop selling a comprehensive range of books on South Africa.* [2 A3]

Hector Pieterson was a 13-year-old schoolboy who was shot and killed during the 1976 Soweto Uprising. His death became both famous and symbolic thanks to a photographer, Sam Nzima, who took a photograph of Mbuyisa Makhubu, another schoolboy carrying Hector Pieterson's body away from the rioting crowd. Sam Nzima was a photographer for the *World Newspaper* which was later banned in 1978, and after the riots he – amongst other photographers that had witnessed and published photographs of the riots – was targeted by police. In 1978 he was put under house arrest at his home near Nelspruit for three months. After years of fighting for the rights to his photograph, *The Star* newspaper finally gave him copyright in 1998.

At the time the compelling and tragic photograph of a lifeless Hector, a horrified Makhubu and Hector's wailing 17-year-old sister running alongside was published worldwide. It showed the world the extremes that the then South African government were capable of in quelling any protest against the apartheid regime – killing defenceless schoolchildren. The 1976 Soweto Uprising began as a peaceful march by students to protest against the Afrikaans language being used as the predominate language for learning and it turned into a bloody riot when the police started shooting. The students gathered along Vilakazi Street next to the Phefeni Junior Secondary School and Orlando West High School with the intention of peacefully marching via the local police station to drop off their petition before continuing on to Orlando Stadium. The intended route was never completed and Hector fell at a spot outside the gates of Orlando West High School on Vilakazi Street. From the shooting site a line of trees symbolising the firing line takes the visitor along Moema Street to the Hector Pieterson Memorial and the museum. A copy of the photograph hangs in the museum, and next to the Hector Pieterson Memorial in the garden in the front of the building. Sam Nzima went on to say, 'I saw a child fall down. Under a shower of bullets I rushed forward and went for the picture. It had been a peaceful march, the children were told to disperse. They started singing Nkosi Sikelele. The police were ordered to shoot.' Nkosi Sikelele, meaning 'God bless Africa', was a protest song in the early years and is now South Africa's national anthem.

The modern red-brick and steel museum which opened in 2004, along with the nearby Hector Pieterson Memorial, has been declared a National Heritage Site for its historical significance. Like the Apartheid Museum, most of the displays are in the way of TV footage and you can look through strategically placed windows to see important sights such as the police station, several schools in Orlando, and the Orlando Stadium where the students intended to finish their peaceful protest on that fateful day. One of the many significant photographs includes that of students carrying a sign saying 'to hell with Afrikaans', and exhibits include original metal dustbin lids which were replaced later by plastic ones in Soweto in the 1980s so they couldn't be used as weaponry (ie: shields). Again, like the Apartheid Museum, there are lots of spaces, and South African visitors are requested to leave behind their experiences and thoughts of the museum; many of them were children involved in the 1976 riots. There are plenty of significant aspects of the memorial itself, a granite slab surrounded by slate walls and a concrete walkway over a water feature. The empty voids between the walls and concrete slabs represent the missing stories and individuals lost in the uprising, the fountain represents rolling tears, and the pieces of rock represent weapons used against the police. The inscription on the memorial reads 'to honour the youth who gave their lives in the struggle for freedom and democracy'.

One of the guides in the museum is Antoinette Sithole, Hector's sister, who was in the photograph running alongside her dead brother. The then 18-year-old

Makhubu who carried Hector's body was also harassed by the police after the riots and he was thought to have gone to Nigeria in 1978 but was never heard from again. Today his mother sells T-shirts at the museum. After the 1994 elections, the 16th June, the day of the uprising, was declared a national holiday – Youth Day in memory of the contribution children made to the struggle against apartheid. Desmond Tutu's church, the Holy Cross Anglican Church, is just behind the memorial, and Walter Sisulu's house is up the street to the left of the museum entrance, though you can't go inside.

JAMES HALL MUSEUM OF TRANSPORT *Pioneers Park (next to Wemmer Pan), Rosettenville Rd, La Rochelle; 1km south of the city centre, take the Mooi St exit off the M2 east, turn right at the T junction and again into Rosettenville Rd; ℡ 011 435 9485–7; www.jhmt.org.za; open Tue–Sun 09.00–17.00; no admission charge, but donations are welcome. There is a museum shop and the Penny Farthing Tuck Shop for drinks and snacks.* [2 D3]

The James Hall Museum of Transport was established by the City of Johannesburg in 1964. The exhibits are of just about every kind of transport there is – ox-wagons, horse-drawn coaches and donkey carts, bicycles and motorbikes, tractors, fire engines, buses, trams, trains and a wide variety of cars. All the vehicles are displayed in big warehouse-style halls or outside under cover. Amongst the collection are some old double-decker trams that were used in Johannesburg's city centre up until 1961.

MANDELA FAMILY MUSEUM *8115 Ngakane St, Orlando West, Soweto;* ✆ *011 936 7754; open daily 09.30–17.00; R20 pp.* [2 A3]

The Mandela Family Museum in Soweto is housed in what was once the home of Nelson Mandela, the world's most famous political prisoner and South Africa's former president. This humble house was Mandela's home from 1946, and it is a tiny place. He originally moved there with his first wife, Evelyn Ntoko Mase, before he married Winnie Madikizela. Mandela himself didn't actually spend a great deal of time living there as he was frequently on the run or had to go into hiding in those early years as a freedom fighter before his arrest and imprisonment in 1962. Winnie lived there with their two daughters and the house was petrol bombed on several occasions and frequently attacked by police.

There are only four rooms and it doesn't take long to look around. Guides will take you through the exhibits, though these are a bit of a mishmash of things, from Mandela's old boots to honorary doctorates presented to him from universities, and a boxing belt given to Mandela by Sugar Ray Leonard (Mandela boxed in his youth). The décor is looking a little worn, but it's not difficult to imagine the family crouched beneath the kitchen table as police fired tear gas at the house, and it demonstrates what a humble beginning one of the world's leading statesmen had. Mandela has received a vast amount of gifts from all over the world. He has always insisted that these are not personal gifts but gifts to the nation, and as such a few are on display in this house (the majority are at the Nelson Mandela Museum in the Eastern Cape province, which is his birthplace). There has recently been much public banter about dropping one of our public holidays (we already have 12) in preparation for Mandela's death, which will of course become Mandela Day. When that day comes the whole of the nation will mourn for Madiba, as he is affectionately called, which is the name of his clan.

When Mandela was released from prison he wanted to go back and live in the house, but this proved impractical. Security was an issue and he only in fact stayed there for 11 days before moving to a larger house in Houghton. Mandela and Winnie separated in 1992 and were divorced in 1998. Mandela married Graça Machel, the widow of the former president of Mozambique, on his 80th birthday in 1998. Winnie set up the museum in 1997, and rather exploited the house to begin with, which included her reaping the benefits of tourists' visits by opening up a restaurant across the road and selling – now a famous story – bottles of Mandela garden soil. The house is now in the hands of the Soweto Heritage Trust.

MUSEUM AFRICA *121 Bree St, Newtown, on Mary Fitzgerald Sq;* ✆ *011 833 5624; open Tue–Sun 09.00–17.00; R7 adults, R2 children and senior citizens. There is guarded parking in Mary Fitzgerald Sq opposite the entrance or behind the Market Theatre complex, and there's a coffee shop and museum shop.* [5 E6]

This is Johannesburg's major history and cultural museum and is housed in the Newtown precinct's old fruit and vegetable market, which was built in 1913 (see page 142 for more information on walking around Newtown). The collections have been accumulated since 1933 by the city library and with funds from the City of Johannesburg, the museum reopened in 1994 as *Museum Africa* in its new home.

There is a huge collection of objects, paintings and photographs telling the story of South Africa. Note that most city tours do stop here but you don't get long, perhaps an hour, and the museum warrants a longer visit to see everything. It is a light and airy building and a good place to while away a few hours. Exhibits are arranged around various themes, from the Stone Age and San rock art to gold mining, township jazz, mock-ups of township shacks, and events during apartheid. Highlights include a shack from the Alexandra township that was previously used as a *shebeen*, with real sounds, shouts, conversations and music recorded during the *shebeen's* happy hour, complete with a baby's wail in the background. There's also a mock-up of a mine tunnel so you can see what hot, confined conditions the miners had to work in. Everything is well displayed in an interactive way with TV footage and music playing, though there are lots of subjects to take in. One of the latest exhibits is on the World Summit on Sustainable Development that took place in Johannesburg in 2002. Also in the museum is the **Bensusan Museum of Photography**. A former mayor of Johannesburg, Dr A D Bensusan, donated his collection to the museum in the 1960s and it includes rare photographic equipment, including a camera dating from 1839, the year photography was invented.

ORIGINS CENTRE *close to the Bertha St entrance to Wits University;* ↘ *011 717 4700; www.origins.org.za; open daily 09.00–18.00 (last ticket 17.00); R45 adults, R2 children. Café with outside terrace and gift shop.* [3 E4]
This is an excellent new museum and for anyone with an interest in the emergence

of mankind in Africa, it thoroughly complements visits to other sites such as Maropeng (see page 211) and the Sterkfontein Caves (see page 215), which make up the recently dubbed Cradle of Humankind region, a World Heritage Site. It was one Raymond Dart, Head of the Department of Anatomy at Wits, who discovered the first *Australopithecus africanus* fossil, dubbed the Taung Child in 1924 in what is now South Africa's North West Province. This discovery led him to believe that mankind originated in Africa and not Europe or Asia as was previously believed and his theory encouraged archaeologists to make further excavations in the region.

This museum, which was opened in 2006 as a result of five years' collaboration with the university and scientists, archaeologists, artists, designers and filmmakers, concentrates on the emergence of mankind in the region. The journey starts with the early archaeological findings, explaining the theory that the origins of humanity are in Africa and that man then spread to the rest of the world, and the exhibits move through rock art, palaeontology, archaeology, genetics, linguistics, symbolism and technology. There are 16 display areas including a courtyard area where there are examples of indigenous plants used as traditional medicine over the centuries, and a wire globe which demonstrates the movement of man from southern Africa to the rest of the world. The displays on the San people (also known as Bushmen) are especially good and include San culture, dance, spirituality and rock art. It is estimated that the San emerged in southern Africa 27,000 years ago, which makes theirs the world's oldest existing human culture, and their rock art the oldest form of communication there is. They are known as 'the people of the eland', and one of the films on exhibit shows the San hunting and killing an eland with poisonous arrows, and there is also a life-sized model of a dying eland in this room. Another film shows the San retreat into their spiritual world through dance, which takes a circular form and is both vivid and disturbing to watch. Amongst the displays are TV screens, and audio devices are given to each visitor for self-guided tours in six languages; English, Afrikaans, Sotho, Zulu, German and French. There are also touch screens where you can email information to your own email address. The final exhibit is on how genetic testing can contribute towards our understanding of ancestry and visitors can test themselves and be added to a world database. This is another of Johannesburg's excellent new museums that exhibits what is an ancient subject but which incorporates interactive and cutting edge technology.

SCI-BONO DISCOVERY CENTRE *Newtown Park;* ℡ *011 639 8400; www.sci-bono.co.za* [5 E6]
This is an interactive centre mainly aimed at schoolchildren in the genres of maths, science, technology and engineering, with companies such as Murray & Roberts hosting displays on construction and the like. At the time of writing it had only just opened so there were very few exhibits, but this will change over time. In the future the centre will also have a career centre for students and a café.

SOUTH AFRICAN BREWERIES (SAB) WORLD OF BEER *15 President St, Newtown;* ℡ *011 836 4900; www.worldofbeer.co.za; open Tue–Sat 10.00–18.00; R10 pp. Tours take 1¹/₂ hrs. Lots of branded T-shirts and other items available in the shop.* [5 E6]

SAB is one of the most successful breweries in the world and now owns most of the local breweries from Cape Town to Cairo, as well as Millers Lite in the US. The SAB Museum traces every aspect of the history and process of brewing beer and a couple of cold ones are included in the price. There are rooms showcasing the very many brands of beer, a mock-up of a traditional *shebeen*, and a honky-tonk pub from a mining camp. The tour guides lead you through 6,000 years of the history of beer, explain about hops and barley in the greenhouse, and demonstrate the brewing process. Interestingly, the World of Beer opened a decade ago at a time when all the other businesses were moving out of the city centre. With the revitalisation of the Newtown precinct, it's now in a prime position, and will appeal to anyone who enjoys the golden nectar. Pub lunches are available in the bar.

SOUTH AFRICAN MUSEUM OF MILITARY HISTORY 22 Erlswold Way, Saxonwold;
☏ 011 646 5513; www.militarymuseum.co.za; open daily 09.00–16.30; R10 adults, R5 senior citizens and children. There is a museum shop and the Vargas Café, named after Alberto Vargas who painted voluptuous women on the noses of World War I planes. [8 B4]

The Museum of Military History, not far from the Johannesburg Zoo, houses all forms of war vehicles and weapons and dads and sons will be happy enough here for the afternoon. It was opened in 1947 by the then Prime Minister, Field Marshall Jan Smuts, to house military items used in World War II. There are fighter planes on display, including a ME262 Swallow that was built by the Germans towards the end of the war and which was the first jet fighter to be built. There are also uniforms, medals and guns, and all up there are over 40,000 exhibits on display. More recently items such as tanks have been added that were used by the South African Defence Force in Angola, and presently a feature on the military wing of the ANC during apartheid is being developed. Very excitingly for me on my visit was to set eyes on the Africa Hinterland Safaris overland truck which is now at the museum. As an ex-overland tour leader I remember seeing this truck, and its crew, on the road as it took tourists up and down Africa, and its story is quite remarkable (see box, page 171). I and my other colleagues in the overland industry certainly had no idea what they were up to!

WITS UNIVERSITY *For more information visit www.wits.ac.za. Take the Empire Rd junction off the M1 and entrances are either off Yale Rd or Bertha St in Braamfontein.* [3 D4]
Short for Witwatersrand, Wits is one of the leading universities in southern Africa and the main 100ha campus is on both sides of the M1 (joined by a bridge) as it goes through Braamfontein. It began life as the South African School of Mines, which was established in Kimberley in 1896 before being moved to Johannesburg in 1904, where it became the Transvaal Technical Institute. In 1922 it was granted university status, and over the years the faculties and the campuses have expanded. Today the university teaches 17,500 students per year and offers more than 3,000 courses. The main campus has attractive pillared Victorian buildings, green lawns and lots of trees. It's a pleasant place to wander around and there are a few things to see. There are

several museums, a planetarium, theatres (listed on page 114) and libraries which altogether hold over a million books. Interesting facts about Wits are that its Bernard Price Institute houses the largest fossil collection in the southern hemisphere, and it has produced four Nobel Prize laureates: Nelson Mandela (peace), Aaron Klug (chemistry), Sydney Brenner (medicine) and Nadine Gordimer (literature).

WORKERS' MUSEUM *52 Jeppe St, Newtown;* ☏ *011 834 1609; open Thu–Sat 09.00–16.00; free* [5 E6]
This museum and library are housed in a national monument that used to be home to approximately 400 municipal workers in 1910 when it was built, and which later went on to become the city's electricity department. The exhibits and photographs demonstrate the iniquitous living conditions of Johannesburg's migrant labour force from the gold-mining days, who played a pivotal role in the growth of the city. One of the most interesting displays is the reconstruction of the conditions in the single-sex hostels in which black miners and workers lived and struggled for the better part of the 20th century. The library boasts an impressive collection of labour-related materials from books, videos and periodicals, chronicling the history of the working-class movement, to economics, labour law and industrial policy.

ZOOLOGY MUSEUM *First floor, Old Education Building, East Campus, Wits University;* ☏ *011 717 6464; open Mon–Fri 08.30–16.30* [3 E4]
This is the only natural history museum in Johannesburg, again popular with school

groups. The usual specimens of bones, skeletons, stuffed fish and birds and shells are displayed in teak cabinets.

ART GALLERIES

THE ABSA GALLERY *ABSA Towers, 160 Main St, city centre;* ☎ *011 350 5139; open Mon–Fri 09.30–15.30; free* [6 H7]
This gallery, at Absa bank's head office, houses around 20,000 pieces of modern South African artwork valued at around R70 million, and it is believed to be the largest corporate art collection in the world. Most of the art is scattered throughout the building in executives' offices and reception areas, though visitors can see some of it in the public areas. The building with its four towers was commissioned in 1999 and as it was being built the architects and artists worked together to make sure the building accommodated the art to its best advantage. One of the most striking exhibits is in the northern towers where at the top of the escalator from the ground floor is a space between the offices that goes up six storeys. Here is a set of carpet banners of giant cartoon-like faces in bright primary colours that hang down the entire six storeys. They are enormous and a great deal of work has gone into them. Also here is an 11m-high wire sculpture of African traditional stools piled on top of each other, and suspended from the ceiling is a metal mobile of the skyline of Johannesburg. Absa sponsors the L'Atelier Award which is open to 21–35-year-old artists and part of the prize is a stay at an

JOZI ART

Other galleries around the city that show changing exhibitions include:

The Premises Johannesburg Civic Centre, Loveday St, Braamfontein; 011 877 6859; www.onair.co.za/thepremises; *open Tue–Sat 12.00–20.00* [4 F4]

The Everard Read Gallery 6 Jellicoe Av, Rosebank; 011 788 4805; www.everard-read.co.za; *open Mon–Fri 09.00–18.00, Sat 09.00–16.00* [8 A2]

Obert Contemporary 14 The High St, Melrose Arch, Melrose; 011 684 1214; www.obertcontemporary.com; *open daily 11.00–19.00* [8 D1]

Goodman GallerY 163 Jan Smuts Av, Parkwood; 011 788 1113; www.goodman-gallery.com; *open Tue–Fri 09.30–17.30, Sat 09.30–16.00* [8 A3]

Gallery on the Square Nelson Mandela Sq, Sandton City, corner 5th and Maude Sts; 011 784 2847; www.galleryonthesquare.co.za; *open Mon–Sat 09.00–18.00* [7 C2]

apartment in *Cité Internationale des Arts* in Paris, an artists' colony where the winner can meet other novices and masters from around the world. Group and solo exhibitions of up-and-coming artists are held throughout the year at the gallery, and you can wander around the public areas and ride the escalators. It's a pleasant experience and you get to witness the bank's employees swish in and out of one of the city's most stylish places to work.

BREAD & BUTTER ✆ *011 880 0250;* e *The Zone@Rosebank; open Mon–Sat 09.00–17.00, Sun 09.00–14.00* [8 B3]
This shop was created by the same guy who started the Young Designers' Emporium (see page 133) and works along the same lines. Local artists 'rent' space in the shop to sell and showcase their work. There are some great contemporary gifts and art on display, such as quirky lamps, pottery, mirrors, jewellery etc and each piece has been individually hand crafted.

COLLECTABLE BOOKS *The Village Mall, 60 Tyrone Av, Parkview;* ✆ *011 646 8320; open Mon–Fri 08.30–17.00, Sat 08.30–13.00*
This is a buyer and seller of antiquarian libraries or single books, maps, share certificates, documents and signatures, and there are prints from 1570 onwards. Also for sale are antiques such as silverware, china, furniture and small oils and watercolours, and the old stamp section is a must for philatelists visiting Johannesburg.

GERTRUDE POSEL GALLERY and the **STUDIO GALLERY** *both in Senate House, Wits University;* ✆ *011 717 1360; open Tue–Fri 10.00–16.00* [3 E4]
The former showcases South African contemporary artists whilst the Studio Gallery exhibits African art and has one of the finest collections of African beadwork in the world.

JOHANNESBURG ART GALLERY *Klein St, Joubert Park;* ✆ *011 725 3130; open Tue–Sat 10.00–17.00; free; gallery shop* [6 G5]
The collection of the city's major public gallery spans international artists such as Rodin, Picasso, Monet and Henry Moore, and many contemporary South African artists. The mining company Anglo American has been involved in sponsorship over the years, which has allowed the gallery to purchase a large range of works of art. Exhibits include 17th-century Dutch paintings, 19th-century British and European work, and later additions include traditional African pieces, such as jewellery made from beads, and sculptures made from wire and metal, amongst other genres. It was first established in 1910 at Wits University and was moved to the three-storey building at Joubert Park in 1915. It's a fine building with sweeping steps and a pillared and frescoed entrance, though there are presently plans to move at least some of the collection to the Turbine Hall in Newtown over the next few years (see page 149). Note that you should exercise caution in the area around Joubert Park as it's in a rough part of the city centre, though Joubert Park has recently been given a facelift, and it's easy enough to drive to and there's secure parking at the gallery.

KIM SACKS GALLERY *153 Jan Smuts Av, Parkwood;* ✆ *011 447 5804; open Mon–Fri 09.00–17.00, Sat 10.00–15.00* [8 A3]
Although African curios can be found at the flea markets, this gallery is a showcase for art from all over Africa. Cloth comes from the Congo and Mali, wooden carvings from west and southern Africa, wire bowls and sculptures from KwaZulu Natal and

there are prints by local artists. There's a huge selection, and although it's not as cheap as the markets, the quality is top notch. Even if you're not buying, a visit here is worthwhile to view the art, and there are changing gallery exhibitions of ceramics or San bushmen art, for example.

MOJAMODERN *167th Av, Parktown North;* ☏ *011 447 9000; www.mojamodern.co.za; open Tue–Fri 11.00–19.00, Sat 10.00–16.00*
This is a gallery of modern art by contemporary artists and there are some superb giant oil paintings on display. The staff are informative and there are new displays every month, and many of the paintings incorporate scenes of modern life in Johannesburg. There are many other galleries and top-of-the-range décor shops along 7th Avenue.

STANDARD BANK GALLERY *corner Simmons and Frederick Sts, city centre;* ☏ *011 631 1889; www.standardbankgallery.co.za; open Mon–Fri 08.00–16.30, Sat 09.00–13.00; free* [6 F7]
Since it opened three decades ago, this gallery has become home to one of South Africa's biggest corporate and African art collections. Standard Bank also decorates their offices around the world with some of their art collection. The gallery hosts exhibitions of local and European contemporary artists and in 2006 hosted an exhibition on Picasso. There are over 5,000 pieces in the African collection, including wood carvings, drums, masks, items of clothing, beads, cloth and ritual objects from all over the continent.

ATTRACTIONS AND PLACES TO VISIT

GOLD REEF CITY *Ormonde, 5km south of the city centre, off the Xavier St exit of the N12 or the Boise's exit of the M2 west, it is clearly signposted;* ℡ *011 248 6800; www.goldreefcity.co.za; open Tue–Sun 09.30–17.00; admission for theme park R70 weekdays, R90 weekends for adults and children, R45 senior citizens, underground tour R60* [2 C3]

Gold Reef City is a re-creation of turn-of-the-20th-century Johannesburg after the discovery of gold in 1886. It is a little sanitised and Disney-like but the main reason for coming here, unless of course you are claustrophobic, is for the opportunity to go down a mine shaft. It is centred around Shaft No 14, which opened in 1897 and closed in 1971, during which time it produced 1.4 million kilograms of gold. It is actually the 13th shaft but they skipped this number due to superstition. Donned with hard hat, torch and battery pack, the underground tour down the mine shaft is lots of fun and very interesting. The mine is a staggering 3,293m deep, though visitors only go down 220m. Mining at such deep levels is very problematic as temperatures rise by 1°C roughly every 33m. In the early years there was no electricity, and lighting underground was by means of candles, which posed a risk of explosions caused by methane gas. Combined with the darkness, the wetness, the heat, the closeness and the ear-shattering noise of the drills, it was a tough way to earn a living for the miners and you can really get a feel of this once underground. The tour takes about half an hour, and as you step out of the lift underground, the first thing you'll see is the whitewashed tunnel. This was painted white to help miners adjust from the darkness of the mine to the brightness outside on their way up at the end of their shift. Given that shifts were often 12 hours' long the miners' eyes were severely affected by the gloom. The tour goes through tunnels supported by gum poles about 2m high, and you'll see the mine manager's station. It was here that the miners deposited their identity cards whilst on shift, and during blasts they would pick them up on the way to the surface. Any cards left would show the manager who was missing. Other exhibits are a dynamite box with a bright red angled lid to prevent miners putting their candles on it and a deafening drill is switched on for five seconds.

Above ground there are replicas of Victorian buildings to look around and most of the staff are dressed in period costume. There's a museum dedicated to gold and you can watch a demonstration of gold pouring. There are also plenty of street performances from robotic shows, clowns and bands to can-can girls, strolling minstrels and gumboot dancers. The latter is a recreational dance originally performed by the miners while still wearing their overalls and gumboots. In the adjoining theme park you can have lots of fun on the roller coasters with names such as Anaconda, Jozi Express and Golden Loop.

Gold Reef City

Miners' Revenge is a water ride, on which you will get wet, and the Tower of Terror is a heart-stopping 47m drop. In addition to all this the Gold Reef City Casino and Apartheid Museum are close by.

JOHANNESBURG ZOO *corner Jan Smuts Av and Upper Park Dr, Parkview;* ⤷ *011 646 2000; www.jhbzoo.org.za; open daily 08.30–17.30, last ticket 16.00; R32 adults, R19 children. If you don't want to walk around you can hire a golf cart.* [2 C1] Set in lovely gardens full of trees and water features and covering 54ha, the Johannesburg Zoo is one of the better of the world's zoos, with spacious enclosures and an impressive collection of animals. It was originally set up in 1904 and many of the first animals were donated by Percy Fitzpatrick, author of the children's book *Jock of the Bushveld,* about his adventures in the bush with his faithful dog. From the outset the zoo was constructed without cages, and animals live in vegetated plots surrounded by moats. There are lions, tigers, elephants, gorillas, chimpanzees, various antelope, the only pair of polar bears in Africa and many other species. There are over 2,000 animals in total and they have been arranged in five zones: The Spice Route (animals found along the old trading routes to India), Heart of Africa (gorillas, chimpanzees and other central African animals), Southern Safari (local southern African animals), Extreme Environments (camels, polar bears, penguins), and Amazonia (animals of South America). There is also a petting farmyard and a number of rides for small children.

In recent years the zoo has been completely refurbished and is a very pleasant

MAX THE GORILLA

One of Johannesburg Zoo's most famous residents was Max the gorilla, who died at the ripe old age of 33 in 2004. Max hit the headlines in 1997 when an armed criminal who was on the run from the police entered his enclosure. Max 'apprehended' the criminal, but was shot and injured twice in the process. After the police caught the man, Max picked up two of the police officers and carried them into his night enclosure – one under each arm! These events earned him the title of Newsmaker of the Year by the Johannesburg Press Club. According to his keeper, Max's favourite food was garlic and he enjoyed the occasional beer.

place to walk around. Educational information boards have been put up explaining about conservation, endangered species and issues that affect the animals in the wild – the bushmeat trade at the chimpanzee enclosure, for example. Special night tours allow visitors to observe the habits of nocturnal creatures and they end with marshmallows and a warming cup of coffee around a bonfire. In fact if you have a tent you're allowed to sleep over in the zoo. There are behind-the-scenes tours that show how the zoo operates. The zoo also hires out small creatures like lizards or spiders to schools for educational purposes.

WORLD OF BIRDS *Montecasino, Fourways; ☎ 011 511 1864; www.montecasino.co.za; open daily 08.30–17.00; Flight of Fantasy bird show, weekdays 11.00 and 15.00, weekends 11.00, 13.00 and 15.00; R25 adults, R15 children under 10 and senior citizens. [1 C2]*

The World of Birds is home to over 1,000 birds from 142 bird species. Most are exhibited in large aviaries enclosing natural vegetation and plenty of trees, though some birds strut across the open lawns or can be seen around the water features. There are paths and boardwalks to take you around and the information about the birds is informative. The highlight here is the Flight of Fantasy show – a free flight demonstration of some of the bigger birds that is really clever and thought to be one of only two shows of its kind in the world (the other one is in Durban). The stars of the show are owls, herons, storks, and birds of prey. Visitors sit in a large amphitheatre facing a stage that is constructed to look like a castle-type building with lots of windows and ledges. The microphoned presenter talks about the birds and as he or she does so, said bird makes its appearance somewhere on the stage. Rather incredibly these birds do exactly as they have been trained and spread their wings, hop to certain ledges or down on the ground, and fly to posts strategically placed around the amphitheatre when prompted by the presenter's voice. The best bit is when the larger eagles fly across the crowd to posts at the top of the amphitheatre, literally just a few centimetres above people's heads. If you're quick you can get a close-up photograph. I have taken small children to see this show and they watched with open mouths. It's magical.

JOHANNESBURG BOTANIC GARDENS *Olifants Rd, Emmarentia;* `011 782 7064;` *www.jobot.co.za; open daily; free* [2 C1]

The 81ha botanic gardens were established in 1968 on the western shore of the lake formed by the Emmarentia Dam perhaps. It is home to over 30, 000 trees, including oaks, Californian redwoods and silver birches. A vast, formal rose garden features some 4,500 roses, and a herb garden includes samples of ancient medicinal herbs used by traditional healers (*sangomas*). The Shakespeare Garden is planted with herbs referred to by Shakespeare in his plays, including mint, camomile, marjoram and lavender. Visitors can picnic on the manicured lawns, and a number of ponds within the garden attract breeding waterfowl, such as the moorhen, crested grebe and Egyptian goose. There are occasional kite flying competitions, and concerts and Shakespeare plays in the attractive open-air amphitheatre.

THE MELVILLE KOPPIES NATURE RESERVE *Melville; entrance at the north end of 3rd Av, Westdene – turn right at the top of Arundel Rd;* `011 482 4797; www.veld.org.za` [2 C1]
This reserve covers 75ha and is split into three sections. The central section (entrance on Judith Rd), Emmarentia, is open to visitors on the first three Sundays of each month, whilst the Louw Geldenhuys view site and the east section is open daily from dawn to dusk and is popular with dog walkers. It is mostly made up of low shrubs and wild fruit trees and in spring many wild flowers appear. The reserve is

home to a number of small mammals such as hares and hedgehogs, reptiles such as lizards and puff adders, and over 200 species of birds have been recorded. It covers a rocky ridge and was declared a national monument in 1963 when an Iron Age furnace was discovered here. Fragments of charcoal, slag, raw iron and broken blowpipes have been excavated and information boards have been put up at the site. There are several paths to follow and maps are available at the gates.

ZOO LAKE *Off Jan Smuts Av, Parkview; open daily; free* [2 C1]

Zoo Lake is a large, lovely well-established park off Jan Smuts Avenue opposite Johannesburg Zoo. Attractions include rowing boats for hire on Zoo Lake itself, a large open-air swimming pool, tennis courts, a bowling club, a tea garden and a couple of restaurants. One of these is Moyo listed under *Eating and Drinking* (see page 96). The park was established in 1904, and even in those early years of Johannesburg's development when blacks and whites lived separately, the city council declared that the park and the neighbouring zoo were open to all races. During apartheid Zoo Lake and the zoo remained open to all. The lake was built in 1908, and in 1937, to commemorate the coronation of King George VI, the Coronation Fountain was built in the middle of it (this is lit up at night). In 1956, as part of Johannesburg's 70th birthday celebration, Margot Fonteyn danced *Swan Lake* in front of the lake. The park is very attractive, with manicured lawns and is full of trees. It's a popular spot for Jo'burgers (especially at the weekends) that come to picnic, jog or mess about in boats. It's particularly popular with the Muslim

GREEN LUNG

A little-known fact about Johannesburg is that it is home to six million trees, and from satellite pictures the city resembles a rainforest. Environmental policies have forbidden building on hills, and this has provided some 4,500 hectares worth of open veld in the form of *koppies* inside the city. When the first Afrikaner farmers arrived the highveld was savannah grassland and there were very few trees. It was these early farmers that planted the first seeds that they had brought up from the Cape, and when the city began to grow, the mining companies planted trees such as blue gum to be used as mining props. Indeed the early miners were paid a penny to plant a sapling. Over the years the city's parks were laid out and planted with pepper trees, and residents planted oaks, jacarandas and plane trees in their gardens. More recently 4,000 trees have been planted in Soweto. The trees attract a large number of birds and Johannesburg is a great spot for birdwatching, even from the garden of your hotel. There are an estimated 420 species of bird present in Gauteng, 60 of which are endemic. The best of the bird books on African birds are *Newman's* and *Robert's* available in the city's bookshops. Bird Life South Africa (↘ 011 789 1122; www.birdlife.org.za) arranges a number of outings in the region.

community, who come here each year to celebrate Eid at the end of Ramadan, and every December a Carols by Candlelight concert is held in the park.

11 Beyond the City

A 30–40-minute drive northwest from Johannesburg will take you through the northern suburbs and into the countryside around the Magaliesberg Mountains and the Hartbeespoort Dam. In this region there are a number of attractions that make for a pleasant distraction from the urban sights. There are a few places to see some of the wildlife South Africa is so famous for, as well as delve into the origins of humankind in an area of Africa that is today believed to be the birthplace of man. Like the other excellent new and modern museums in the city, this area has witnessed great investment in its tourism industry and there are some wonderful new attractions to visit. The best way to explore is with a car, though most of the tour operators listed on page 68 can arrange half- or full-day trips.

DE WILDT CHEETAH FARM *on the R513 approx 15km east of Hartbeespoort;*
☎ *012 504 1921; www.dewildt.org.za; tours operate on Tue, Thu, Sat and Sun, 10.00 and 13.30; R165 pp, no children under 6yrs; limited numbers so booking is essential.*
The De Wildt Cheetah Centre was established in 1971 with the aim of breeding cheetah, which at the time numbered only about 800 in South Africa. Since then over 750 cubs have been born at the centre, including the rare king cheetah, and this

has been one of the world's most successful breeding projects for cheetah. Thanks to their efforts, the cheetah was taken off South Africa's list of endangered species in 1986. They have also contributed to our understanding of cheetah and proved that cheetah bred in captivity do not lose their hunting instinct and are capable of adapting quickly to natural environments. The centre now breeds other rare and endangered species such as brown hyena, suni antelope, blue and red duiker, bontebok, and vultures, including the rare Egyptian vulture. To date over 500 wild dogs have been born at the centre and many of these have been released into the large game parks such as Kruger and Madikwe. The tour begins with a 20-minute talk about the history of the centre, the genetics of cheetah, and the centre's various conservation success stories, followed by a $2^{1}/_{2}$-hour game drive around the spacious enclosures in open-topped game vehicles. If there are small cubs, you may be able to pet them, and for an extra fee you can have a photo taken with one of the four trained cheetahs. The guides, some of them volunteers, are very enthusiastic and clearly love what they do.

ELEPHANT SANCTUARY *2km from the Damdoryn Crossroad (see page 208) on the Rustenberg road; ✆ 012 258 0423; www.elephantsanctuary.co.za. Admission R385 adults, R195 children (lunch extra); and 14.00–16.45 (or extra to stay until 21.00 for dinner), R385 adults, R195 children; elephant riding R350 adults, R250 children over 8yrs; booking essential. Tours daily at 08.00–09,45, R325 adults, R195 children; 10.00–1300. The sanctuary also offers overnight stays; contact them for details.*

The newish Elephant Sanctuary is home to six elephants in a tract of natural indigenous bush where there are a number of elephant interactive programmes on offer. This is the sister operation of the successful elephant sanctuary near Plettenberg Bay on the Garden Route. All the programmes include a 200m walk with the elephants, during which if the elephants are feeling friendly they will let you hold on to their trunks. There's also the opportunity to feed them, and the guides will explain elephant behaviour and tell you about each individual's personality and history. On hot days you may get to see the elephants in the waterhole, and if you opt to stay for dinner you'll also get to see them put to bed in their stables. This is an ideal way to get close up to elephants and children will love the experience.

HARTBEESPOORT DAM AND MAGALIESBERG MOUNTAINS *www.hartbeespoortdam.com, www.magaliesinfo.co.za*

The manmade Hartbeespoort Dam is 60km northwest of Johannesburg in the heart of the Magaliesberg Mountains. For city dwellers there are a number of attractions and the mountains and dam are popular as a recreational and hiking retreat for urbanites seeking fresh air at the weekends throughout the year. The dam was originally built in 1923 where the Crocodile River cuts through the mountains, and the dam wall was further raised in the 1970s. The water is channelled to irrigate farms in the region and it's also very popular for watersports. The Magaliesberg Mountains run east to west over about 160km and in 1977, along with the dam, they were declared a Natural Heritage Site. The unusual name of the mountains is in fact meaningless as when the Voortrekers arrived they named them after a local chief who was called Mohale, but they mis-spelt his name. The early Voortrekers, or Boers, first settled in the valleys of the Magaliesberg as farmers after they had trekked up from the Cape. During the Anglo–Boer War the Boers, who were very familiar with the mountains, used secret pathways to cross them and launch attacks on the British soldiers. The British built blockhouses as look-out posts to restrict the movement of the Boer soldiers and ruins of these can still be seen on the tops of the mountains.

The highest peak is 1,850m above sea level, but because of the fairly high altitude of the region, the mountains rise no more than 400m above the landscape. They offer non-strenuous hiking and walking amongst the gently sloping meadows and sandstone cliffs and there are many country hotels in the region offering a number of activities. The slopes and summits are richly wooded and numerous streams have their source on the ridge, and tobacco and citrus and tropical fruits are grown in the valleys amongst the foothills. The mountains' ledges are important breeding grounds for the endangered Cape vulture, and it is also a destination popular with hang-gliders and para-gliders. The vultures are known to be so used to the artificial 'birds' they launch off the cliffs and fly in perfect synchronisation with them.

Although the featureless regional towns do not hold much appeal, the highlight of this area is to escape to the mountains and play on or around the dam. However most of Gauteng wants to do exactly this and during weekends the region gets horribly crowded, when traffic chokes the country roads and armadas of jet skis take to the water. If you are planning a visit, then consider going mid-week. The best way to explore is by car and you can pick up a *Magaliesberg Meander* map at a number of venues, including the tourist offices (*www.magaliesmeander.co.za*). The R24 and the R560 run along the south of the mountains whilst the N4 runs along the north. There are plenty of distractions along the way such as country hotels, coffee shops and tea gardens, a variety of shops catering for day trippers selling anything from crafts to homemade jam, and a few places to visit. The road through Hartbeespoort follows the northern lakeshore before crossing the dam and rejoining the N4. At the junction after crossing the dam, known as the Damdoryn Crossroad, is an enormous African curio market, and the Welwitschia Country Market with 38 shops selling arts and crafts, clothing, jewellery and ceramics, a children's fairground, and three restaurants (✆ 083 302 8085; *www.countrymarket.co.za*; open Tue–Sun, and all public holidays 09.00–17.00).

Another way to see the Magaliesberg Mountains is from a hot-air balloon, and Bill Harrop's Original Balloon Safaris (✆ 011 705 3201; *www.balloon.co.za*) offer daily 1hr flights over the mountains at sunrise, which include a champagne breakfast.

HARTBEESPOORT DAM SNAKE AND ANIMAL PARK *in the village of Hartbeespoort on the northern lakeshore; ✆ 012 253 1162; open daily 08.00–17.00, snake feeding Sat–Sun 12.00, seal show Sat–Sun 15.00; R50 adults, R20 children, under 3 free; pleasure boat cruises on the lake depart regularly throughout the day.*
This is basically an old-fashioned zoo on the lakeshore, and whilst there is an

impressive collection of animals, including lions, tigers, panthers, cheetahs, pumas, leopards, jaguars, chimpanzees, orang-utans, and a very large collection of reptiles and snakes, the enclosures are cramped and old and there are far better places to see animals in Africa. Nevertheless the animals seem to be well looked after, and children especially will enjoy seeing so many species; it's just a shame they are not housed in more spacious and natural environments.

KRUGERSDORP GAME RESERVE *off the R24 to the west of Krugersdorp;* ✆ *011 950 9900; www.afribush.co.za; open daily 08.00–18.00; R40 adults, R20 children under 12*
This is a private game reserve and a similar set up to Rhino and Lion Nature Reserve (page 213). It covers 1,500ha and although fairly small is home to around 30 mammal species, including white rhino, buffalo, giraffe, hippo, wildebeest, zebra, hyena, jackal and several antelope species, including the rare roan and sable antelope, and there is a separate 100ha lion enclosure. The reserve has several different habitats including grassland, rocky outcrops and forest, and, as well as the game, over 200 species of birds have been recorded here. You can drive yourself around (all the roads are tarred) or two-hour guided game drives are on offer. There's a pleasant picnic site with two swimming pools near the entrance and accommodation is available.

LESEDI CULTURAL VILLAGE *on the R512 towards Hartbeespoort Dam;* ✆ *012 205 1394; www.lesedi.com; tours daily 11.30, 16.30; R285 pp, under 12 half price, under 5 free; booking essential*

Wooden mask

Here there are traditional family units built in mock-up villages from various South African tribes: Zulu, Pedi, Xhosa and Basotho. A guide will take you around and show you traditional ways of life, dress and music, cooking and eating, and farming, food gathering and storage, and everything is demonstrated by the staff in their traditional dress. This is very touristy, but is nevertheless a professional and interesting set up, and the staff are wonderful; very theatrical and friendly and the whole place is vibey and colourful. There is a choice of two daily programmes and if you don't have transport the tour operators can arrange visits here. The first is the lunchtime excursion, known as the Monati Experience, which starts at 11.30. On arrival you are given a welcome drink and have the opportunity to browse in the curio shop, before watching a short film about the origins of South Africa's peoples. This is followed by a tour of the homesteads and a display of singing and dancing which really is quite infectious, and is finished off by a buffet lunch of African delicacies at the Nyama Choma restaurant. The evening programme, the Boma Experience, is the same and starts at 16.30 and ends with dinner. The latter is probably the better as fires are lit and the restaurant is quite atmospheric at night. You can also stay overnight in the Protea Hotel-run traditional *bomas* decorated with crafts.

THE LION PARK *close to Lanseria Airport, off the R512;* ☏ *011 460 1814; www.lion-park.com; open daily 08.30–17.00 winter, 08.30–18.00 summer; R65 adults, R45 children 4–12, free for under 4s, small extra fee to visit the cub enclosure, R100 pp for a guided tour*

This park is home to over 80 lions, including cubs and white lions, as well as a number of other species such as hyena, wild dog, cheetah, zebra, giraffe and some antelope. The park was first established in 1966 by the world-famous Chipperfields Circus but has been under new management since 1999. The animals live in spacious drive-through enclosures covering 208ha, and visitors can drive around themselves or park up in the car park and jump on one of the park's vehicles for a guided tour. The tracks around the park are well maintained and suitable for a normal car. Be warned though; keep your windows up as the lions do not think twice about coming up to the cars (on my visit a large male licked the rain off my wing mirror). Back at the visitors' centre, which has a shop and restaurant, you can visit Cub World to pick up and play with the cubs or feed a giraffe between 12.00 and 15.00. It's great for kids and for those short of time and not going on safari in South Africa.

MAROPENG *7km from the Sterkfontein Caves on the R24 towards the Magaliesberg Mountains;* ☏ *011 668 3200; www.discover-yourself.co.za; open daily 09.00–17.00; R65 adults, R35 children; tours are self-guided, and you can go through the attraction at your own pace; allow at least 2hrs.* There are three restaurants on site, some curio/gift shops at the entrance and a 24-room hotel.

Maropeng is a brand new 260m² exhibition centre that was officially opened by President Mbeki in 2005 and the whole initiative is very impressive. It's an interactive exhibition space and museum that literally takes you through the journey of mankind from the beginnings of earth to where we are at today. At the entrance are four stark concrete pillars bearing the orange logo of Maropeng, which means 'returning to the place of origin' in *Setswana*. The centre, which is housed in an imposing, partly disguised grassy mound 20m high and 35m wide, was designed to look like an ancient burial mound from the front and a very modern architectural structure at the rear, which symbolises the journey through time. The history of our world and humankind as a species is brought to life by audiovisual techniques, sound effects, theme-park technology and interactive displays, and it's marvellously clever and very hi-tec.

The first exhibit is a boat ride, which takes you through a series of tunnels of artificial rock accompanied by strange prehistoric sounds and swirls of orange and red mist. This represents the basic elements that make up our world – water, air, fire and earth, and the ride takes you past waterfalls and icebergs, into the eye of a storm, past erupting volcanoes and at the end you are deposited at the beginning of the world. Here is a projected globe of the earth which tells the story from the time that gases formed to create planets 4.6 billion years ago to the formation of the continents. Naturally there is a 'path to humanity' display with a line of apes to man gradually standing up and becoming taller, and a number of exhibits of fossils and the history of archaeology in the region. There are also a number of interactive displays throughout the exhibition space, including one with phones you can pick up and hear stories about extinct animals such as the *dodo* or *quagga*. The commentary is delightful – the woolly mammoth speaks in an eastern European accent. The displays move through human development, how humans have changed the world, environmental and natural disasters, and population and global appetite. Interestingly in the population section, it claims that by 2025 over half of Africans will be living in cities. Towards the end of the journey is a wonderful display of photographs of faces from all the races in the world, and a series of mesmerising images are projected onto a large screen to demonstrate the achievements of man. These include archive footage of Charlie Chaplin films, images of food, famous travel monuments, streets and ordinary people, and cover the creativity of human beings in art, design, transport, dance, surgery, man on the moon, music etc and the film ends with (rather predictably) an atom bomb going off. It's quite a fabulous experience and is recommended for young and old. Darwin would have been most impressed by this dedication to the theory of evolution.

RHINO AND LION NATURE RESERVE *from the N14 Krugersdorp–Pretoria road, turn off at the Kromdraai sign and follow the signposts for approx 7km;* \ *011 957 0106; www.rhinolion.co.za; open daily 08.00–15.45, lion feeding 15.00 on Sat and Sun; R70 adults, R30 children; guided tours run from the reception area and last for around 2¹/₂hrs.* The Rhino and Lion Nature Reserve is a privately owned nature reserve that covers about 1,600ha. It is not too far from Johannesburg, but far enough to make you feel you are out in the bush. The lions are in a spacious fenced area and the best time to

CRADLE OF HUMANKIND

🔈 *011 355 1200; www.cradleofhumankind.co.za*

The Cradle of Humankind is a valley covering 47,000ha roughly 40km west of Johannesburg. It is the location of over 40 different fossil sites where several of the world's most famous and important fossils have been discovered. Tens of thousands of hominid and animal fossils and stone tools have been excavated, and 40% of the entire world's human ancestor fossils have been found in this region; work is ongoing today. The area was declared a World Heritage Site in 1999, and whilst most of the sites are on privately owned land, any finds belong to the world. You can visit Sterkfontein and Maropeng (below) and also visit the newly opened Origins Centre at Wits University in the city (see page 186) for a full low-down on how this little corner of southern Africa is now generally regarded as the birthplace of humankind and how it was Africans that went on to populate the rest of the earth. Johannesburg may be a young city, but its earliest residents were in the neighbourhood over four million years ago.

see them is during feeding times. Other animals include rhino, buffalo, cheetah, wild dog, hippo and crocodile, and the newly built breeding centre houses Bengal and Siberian tigers, jaguars and white lions. The reserve was founded in 1985 by Ed Hern, a stockbroker, and from a modest beginning of two white rhinos and some antelope species, the reserve now boasts 600 head of game from 25 different species. Emphasis has also been placed on breeding and 11 white rhino calves have been born at the reserve to date. The staff also feed vultures each day, which fly in from the Magaliesberg Mountains to the 'vulture restaurant'.

Also in the park is the Wonder Cave, one of the archaeological sites that make up the Cradle of Humankind. Like the Sterkfontein Caves, it was discovered about a hundred years ago by early gold miners looking for limestone, which was harvested for gold and used to make cement. The cave is thought to be about 1.5 million years old, it stretches 150m across and is just over 120m long. There are several stalactite and stalagmite formations, though some of these were lost during early mining activities. At the bottom of the cave is a small lake, which usually only appears in the wet season. Tours are conducted every hour.

Facilities at the park include individual *braai* areas, a kiosk, curio shop, swimming pool, volleyball court and the Crocodile Pub, where visitors can enjoy a drink whilst watching the crocodiles at close range. Accommodation is also available in chalets or a tented camp – check out the website for details.

STERKFONTEIN CAVES *50km west of the city on the Krugersdorp–Hekpoort road (R563);* ℡ *011 956 6342; www.sterkfontein-caves.co.za; open daily, tours run every half hour from 09.00–16.00; R15 adults, R7 children*
The Sterkfontein Caves were discovered in 1896 by a prospector looking for lime for use in the gold mining industry, and, as the limestone was removed, older rock

was exposed underneath. Since then over 500 fossils and over 9,000 stone tools have been found in the caves but they are most famous for two world-renowned hominid finds: the fossilised remains of Mrs Ples that were discovered in 1947 and which date back 2.5 million years (though more recently it is suspected that she is actually Mr Ples); and Little Foot discovered in 1995, which is an almost complete ape-like skeleton believed to be between 3.3 and 4.1 million years old, of which parts are still being removed from the caves. Mrs Ples was originally

Mr/Mrs Ples

named after *Plesianthropus africanus* meaning 'almost human' but was later identified as *Australopithecus africanus,* whose features include a more globular cranium and less primitive teeth and face. Although not completely identified, it is thought that Little Foot is also *Australopithecus africanus* and is the oldest item recovered in the Cradle of Humankind and one of the oldest hominid fossils in the world.

A new interactive centre opened in 2005, which is a sleek block on concrete stilts, with a shop, a restaurant with views across the countryside and an exhibition centre. Here you learn about early humans and their evolution, before a guide collects you for a tour of the caves. There are walkways over the excavation sites and then you go underground past the spectacular eroded shapes of dolomite, through the vast chamber to an underground lake with its tranquil, crystal-clear waters that extends some distance into the unexplored chambers. Sadly many of the cave's stalactites and stalagmites were removed or damaged by early limestone mining activities at the beginning of the 20th century.

WALTER SISULU NATIONAL BOTANICAL GARDEN *end of Malcolm Rd, Poortview, Roodepoort approx 25km to the west of Sandton, take the Beyers Naude exit off the N1 and follow the R564;* ☏ *011 958 1750; www.nbi.ac.za/sisulu; open daily 08.00–18.00, no entry after 17.00; R15 adults, R7 children, under 6s free, free entrance for senior citizens on Tue; restaurant, gift and book shop*

This botanical garden was previously called the Witwatersrand National Botanical Garden and was renamed after the activist Walter Sisulu's death. It covers about 300ha and consists of both landscaped and natural areas and the highlight is the Witpoortjie Waterfall, which tumbles dramatically over a cliff. The vegetation includes about 600 species of indigenous trees and plants, including grand oaks and cherry trees, and the nursery has over 2,500 species of succulents. There are plenty of pleasant walks through the gardens which are lovingly tended, and in the wetland area is a boardwalk leading to a bird hide. A breeding pair of black eagles nest on the cliffs alongside the waterfall and along with over 220 bird species, there are also a number of reptiles and small mammals, including small antelope and jackal. The ponds and streams attract water birds such as Egyptian geese and yellowbilled ducks.

12 Language

There are 11 official languages in South Africa; *English, Zulu, Xhosa, Afrikaans, Venda, Swazi, North Sotho, South Sotho, Tswana, Sindebele* and *Shangaan*; all of which are spoken in Johannesburg. However English is by far the predominant language of government, business and the media, and can be understood by most people. Road signs are mainly in both English and Afrikaans. As well as English, *izulu* (Zulu) is the most widely spoken language, which is used by 21% of Johannesburg's residents and 36% of Africans. Afrikaans is used by 17% of all residents, more than two-thirds (68%) of coloureds and more than half (56%) of whites. There are also significant numbers of Portuguese speakers from neighbouring Portuguese-speaking African countries, growing numbers of French speakers from west and central Africa, and the Indian and Chinese communities speak their home languages.

Another unusual language unique to South Africa, and then only to the gold and diamond mines of early Johannesburg, is *Fanalago*. This is a language created because miners came to the mines with 50 different languages and had to have a means of understanding and communicating with one another when working. It is based mostly on Zulu vocabulary, with some words from English, Afrikaans and Portuguese.

Developed in 1910, it consists of 2,000 words, 500 of them swear words, and it was thought to be insulting to use it above the ground!

Whilst you will hear English everywhere, you may come across some words you've never heard before. Some Afrikaans, African and slang words pepper South Africans' speech when talking in English and these words are uniquely South African.

Ag Usually used at the beginning of a sentence to indicate irritation or shame, as in 'Ag no man!'

Babbelas Hangover

Bakkie Small pick-up truck

Biltong A South African favourite snack of dried and salted meat

Boet Afrikaans word for brother, used as a term of affection amongst men. Also refers to a pot or beer belly.

Boerewors Traditional spicy South African sausage also referred to as *wors*.

Braai Popular South African version of a barbecue. Traditionally *boets* will stand around the *braai* and cook the *wors* with a beer in hand, whilst the women make the salads. *Braaing* is most definitely a man's prerogative.

Broeks Seems to describe any garment worn around the rear end – swimming trunks, shorts, pants, knickers or briefs

Bru A term of affection used amongst men similar to *boet*, 'Hey, my bru, howzit?'

China A term of affection meaning good friend, 'Howzit, my china?'. Again a word used amongst men.

Cool drink This is the common term for a fizzy drink (or soda) such as Coca-Cola. (Ask for a soda in South Africa and you will get soda water.)

Dinges (Sounds like 'ring us') Used when someone can't immediately remember the name of a person or object, *'When is dinges coming around?'*; similar to whatsizname.

Doll Popular expression of affection amongst Sandton housewives in Johannesburg's northern suburbs. Usually pronounced *doooollll*...

Dop or **doppie** Drink, usually alcoholic. *'It's six o'clock, so it must be time for a doppie.'*

Dorp Village or small town. Usually used to describe somewhere with only one set of traffic lights and a few farmers walking around.

Dumpie A South African beer served in a brown 340ml bottle.

Graze Eat or food

Hap Bite, *'Take a hap of this'*

Howzit A slang South African greeting

Izzit An expression frequently used in conversation and equivalent to *'is that so?'*

Ja well no fine A mix of Afrikaans and English, it is used to express a sense that things aren't really fine but there's not much you can do about it.

Joll Roughly translated as party. *'Let's go for a joll'* would mean *'Let's go for a night out'*, though it can refer to anything from a picnic to an all-night rave.

Just now If a South African tells you they will do something *'just now'*, they mean they will do it in the near future but not immediately. If they tell you *'now now'* then they will do it immediately.

Koki A coloured marker or felt-tip pen

Koppie A small hill

Lappie A cloth used for various cleaning purposes

Lekker Afrikaans word meaning nice. It is often used in association with food, *'That wors is lekker'*.

Madiba The name used by many South Africans when speaking about former president Nelson Mandela. It is used affectionately, but is actually the name of his clan. It is so widely used that even the media refer to Mandela as Madiba.

Naartjie The South African name for a tangerine.

Oke A colloquial reference to a man, similar to chap or bloke.

Pap A stiff porridge made from maize flour and a staple all over Africa.

Pasop Afrikaans word meaning watch out. Seen on Beware of the Dog signs.

Potjiekos A three-legged cast iron pot used for cooking over a fire.

Robot South Africans tend to refer to traffic lights as robots.

Rooibos A popular South African tea made in the Cape.

Rooinek Taken from the Afrikaans this translates as red neck, but does not mean the same as it does in the United States. It was first used by Afrikaners many decades ago to refer to Englishmen, because of the way their white necks would turn pink from sunburn. Today it is often used by Afrikaans speakers as a term of affection towards English speakers.

Scale To scale something means to steal it. If someone is scaly then he or she is not a person that you would trust.

Shame Unlike elsewhere in the world, this is an expression that broadly denotes sympathetic feeling. For example, when admiring a puppy one might say, *'Ag shame!'* which would express that the puppy was cute.

Shebeen Township pub. They used to be illegal unlicensed places often at the back of someone's home, but these days they are fully legal informal pubs and the focal meeting places in the townships.

Sis *'That's sis man!'* describes an object or act that is particularly disgusting or vulgar.

Skinner Gossip. Someone who talks behind someone's back is known as a *skinnerbek*.

Skrik Fright. *'I caught a big skrik when that car pulled out suddenly.'*

Slops Sandals or flip-flops worn to the beach

Spanspek South African word for cantaloupe melon. Any request for a cantaloupe is likely to be met with a blank stare.

Stoep Best described as a veranda or terrace but covers any enclosed area in front of a house. All South Africans enjoy a *doppie* on their *stoep*.

Struesbob ('It's true as bob' – spoken very fast) It's the gospel truth.

Tackies Running shoes or trainers

Tannie This Afrikaans word literally means auntie, but is used by Afrikaners as a sign of respect for any woman who is ten or more years older than themselves.

Traffic circle Roundabout

Van der Merwe Van der Merwe is the butt of many a South African joke, much like Paddy is in Irish jokes. He is a sort of not very bright farmer type.

Vrot Afrikaans for rotten. *'This egg is vrot'*. Alternatively, it can be used to describe something as smelly: *'Put your tackies back on, they're vrot'*.

Where do you stay? Literally translates as *'where do you live?'*

Your side/my side *'What's happening your side?'*, *'Why don't you come over to my side?'* This basically generally refers to where you or the other person you are talking to is actually located at the time of asking, without specifically stating where that location might be.

13 Further Information

BOOKS

There are dozens of interesting books on Johannesburg and Exclusive Books has excellent travel, coffee-table books and Africana sections.

Accone, Darryl *All Under Heaven* David Philip, 2004. This is a beautifully written book which tells the story of the author's Chinese–South African family living in Johannesburg and Pretoria over three generations from the early 1900s to today. It recounts the difficulties faced in the gold-mining town of the early 20th century, and later, in apartheid South Africa.

Alfred, Mike *Johannesburg Portraits* Jacana, 2003. This is a stylish coffee-table book showcasing famous former residents of Johannesburg, and it's illustrated by sketches. It looks at turn-of-the-century rand lords and architects, ANC stalwarts Walter and Albertina Sisulu, palaeontologist and scientist Phillip Tobias, and diva Sibongile Khumalo, amongst others. Every story tells the reader as much about the city's political and social history as it does about each vibrant personality.

Bremner, Lindsay *Johannesburg, One City, Colliding Worlds* STE Publishers, 2004. Lindsay Bremner, professor of architecture at Wits University, wrote five essays for The Sunday Times in early 2002. Now in a book they are told in eloquent style, and give the reader a gritty look at the city in the 21st century. She looks at the demise of the city centre and examines the goal of transforming it again into a world-class city.

Cohen, David *People Who Have Stolen From Me* Picador Africa, 2004. This is a novel which serves as a study of Johannesburg's inner city street life. The story is centred around Jules Street and is about two friends who own Jules Street Furnishers. It describes the challenges of dealing with defaulting customers, hiring former car jackers as repossession agents, and gangs robbing and defrauding their business.

Holland, Heidi and Roberts, Adam (eds) *From Jo'burg to Jozi* Penguin, 2002 and

Roberts, Adam and Thloloe, Joe (eds) *Soweto Inside Out* Penguin, 2004

These are very readable collections of stories from a variety of writers and journalists who were asked to write 1,000 words about Johannesburg or Soweto – all profits from the books go towards AIDS charities. There are all sorts of subjects from memoirs, historical essays and amusing anecdotes to quirky comments about living in the city, and the stories reflect the changes that the city has witnessed over the decades.

Magubane, Peter *Soweto* Struik, 2001. Well-known photographer Peter Magubane has captured the many emotions of Soweto; anguish, happiness, frustration, hard work, exhaustion and joy. This coffee-table book is jam-packed with his mostly colour photographs and leaves the reader with a pretty accurate feel for what life in Soweto is like.

Rubin, Nadine and Temkin, Nikki *Chic Jozi, the Jo'burg pocketbook* Struik, 2005. This is a cute little book written by two *dolls* from the northern suburbs. It highlights all the chic and happening things going on in the city, covering just about everything from where to buy the best wallpaper or flowers, to the best caterers and spas, and where to go to do belly dancing or martial arts.

Tillim, Guy *Jo'burg* STE Publishers, 2005. This is a collection of photographs of inner city images by Guy Tillim. He captures the faces of black tenants and their hard lives in the city's high rises, which were vacated in the 1980–90s by retreating whites.

MAPS

Johannesburg Tourism (see page 30) issues good and compact maps of the city – contact them in advance and they will post them to you. If you are driving it is essential to carry a comprehensive road map. There are several available in all branches of Exclusive Books and at many of the larger petrol stations. These are published by Map Studio and the AA amongst others, and Engen petrol stations produce their own one. Most of these have good street maps as well as driving maps of Gauteng's highways, with information about exit ramps, mileage and interchanges. If you need detailed information about all of Johannesburg's suburbs, the Map Studio (*www.mapstudio.co.za*) produces a number of fat street atlases.

WEBSITES

As well as the tourism authority websites listed on page 30, the City of Johannesburg (*www.joburg.org.za*) has an excellent website with thousands of pages that cover everything from how to pay your rates bill to history, culture, events, eating out, accommodation and useful telephone numbers. The writers have especially concentrated on the city council's objectives and progress in its many projects to improve the city. www.joburg.co.za has general tourist information and is up to date with listings and events, and www.tonight.co.za features celebrity gossip and what's on, including the movie, TV and radio schedules.

WIN £100 CASH!

READER QUESTIONNAIRE

Complete and return this questionnaire for the chance to win £100 cash in our regular draw

(Entries may be posted or faxed to us, or scanned and emailed.)

Your feedback is important. To help us plan future guides please answer all the questions below. All completed questionnaires will qualify for entry in the draw.

Have you used any other Bradt Guides? If so, which titles?.....................

....

What other publisher's travel guides do you use regularly?.....................

Where did you buy this guidebook?..

What was the main purpose of your trip to Johannesburg (or for what other reason did you read our guide)? eg: holiday/business/charity etc. ....

What other destinations would you like to see covered by a Bradt guide?

....

Would you like to receive our catalogue/e-newsletter?

YES/NO (please give details) . . . .

If yes – by post or email? . . . .

Your age   16–25 □   26–45 □   46–60 □   60+ □

Male/Female (delete as appropriate)

Home country. . . . .

Please send us any comments about this guide or other Bradt Travel Guides. . . . . .

. . . .

. . . .

. . . .

. . . .

. . . .

. . . .

. . . .

**For a current list of titles and prices, please see our
website – www.bradtguides.com, or call us for a catalogue.**

Order Form

Please send me one copy of the following guide at **half the UK retail price**

Title   *Retail price*   *Half price*

. . . .

Post & packing (£1/book UK; £2/book Europe; £3/book rest of world)   . . . .

Total   . . . .

Name. . . . .

Address . . . .

Tel . . . .   Email . . . .

☐ I enclose a cheque for £ . . . . made payable to Bradt Travel Guides Ltd

☐ I would like to pay by credit card. Number: . . . .

Expiry date . . . . . . / . . . . 3-digit security code (on reverse of card)

☐ Please add my name to your mailing/e-newsletter list. (For Bradt use only.)

☐ I would be happy for you to use my name and comments in Bradt marketing material.

Send your order on this form, with the completed questionnaire, to:

Bradt Travel Guides/JOH
23 High Street, Chalfont St Peter, Bucks SL9 9QE
☏ +44 (0)1753 893444   f +44 (0)1753 892333
e info@bradtguides.com   www.bradtguides.com

Index